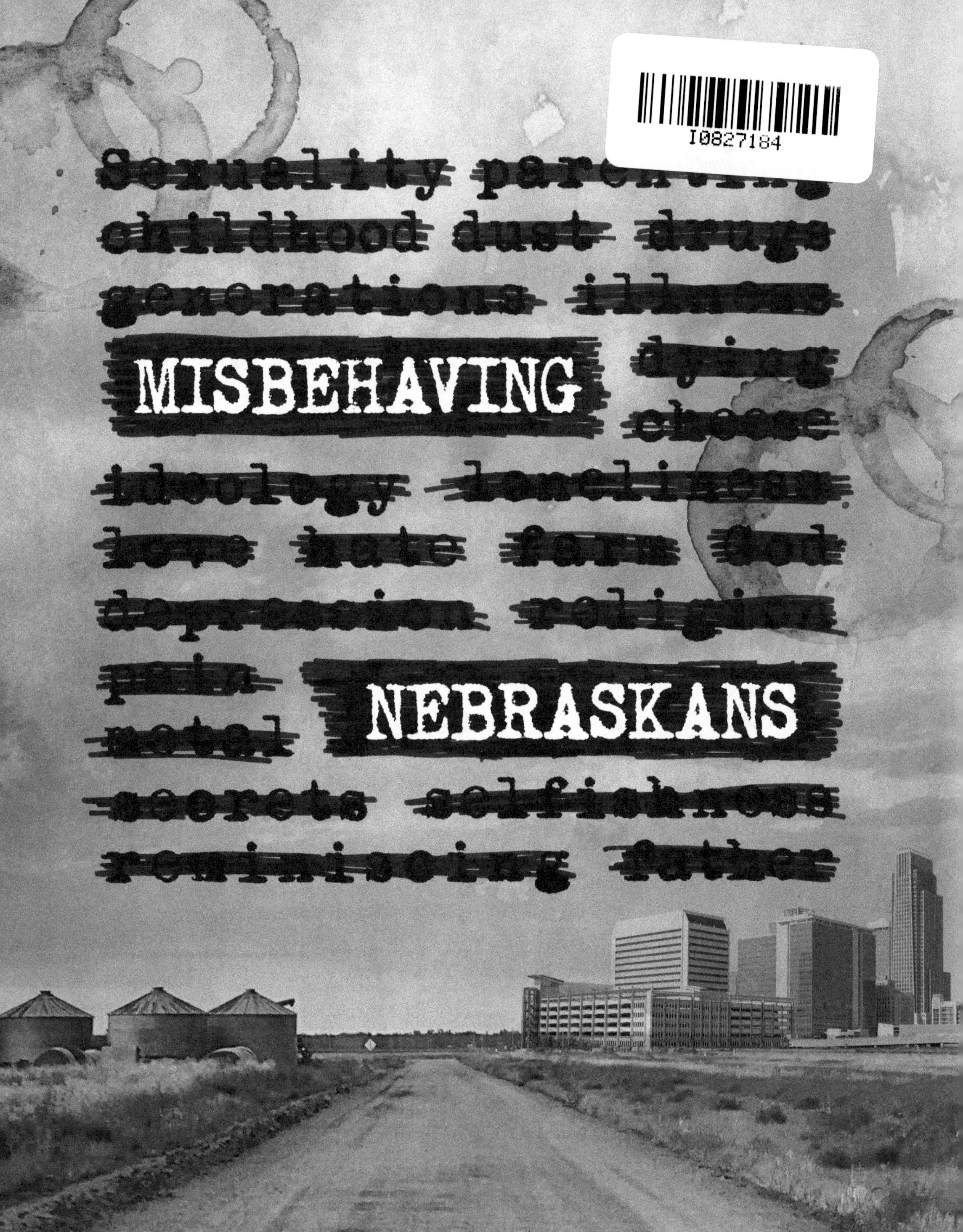
MISBEHAVING
NEBRASKANS

COMPILED BY
CONCIERGE MARKETING, INC.

concierge
marketing inc.
PUBLISHING SERVICES

Omaha, Nebraska

To those clients who have continually championed us, heralded us, and encouraged us.
To the amazing writers and artists who participated, all of you are an inspiration.
To our friends and Nebraskans who are living the good life.

Published by:
Concierge Marketing, Inc.
4822 South 133rd Street
Omaha, NE 68137
www.ConciergeMarketing.com
402-884-5995

Paperback Color ISBN: 978-1-945505-57-7
Paperback B&W ISBN: 978-1-945505-58-4
Hardcover Color ISBN: 978-1-945505-59-1
Kindle ISBN: 978-1-945505-60-7
EPUB ISBN: 978-1-945505-61-4

Library of Congress Control Number: 2017961223
Library of Congress Cataloging data on file with the publisher.

Thank you to:
Marilyn June Coffey, for her inspiration and gusto for this anthology.
Rachel Moore for her stunning book design and passion about this project.
Ellie Godwin for her keen organization and swaggy juggling of the entrants and winners.
Lisa Pelto for pushing this over the finish line with a lot of sweat, a few tears, and even a drop of blood.
Sandra Wendel for her constant encouragement, skill, and cheerleading.
Sarah for researching and composing the judging criteria and oversight of the mountain of entries.
Erin for her editorial assistance and willingness to put a critical eye to the work of newbies and experts alike.
The many friends, readers, and book lovers whose enthusiasm has been unwavering about this book.

Printed in the United States of America.
10 9 8 7 6 5 4 3

Contents

Look for these seals that signify the award winners selected by the judges.

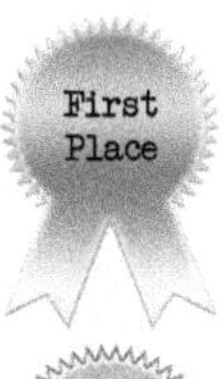

The Merry Widower
Robert Mundy

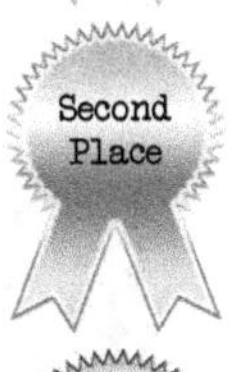

The Provocateur
Marilyn June Coffey

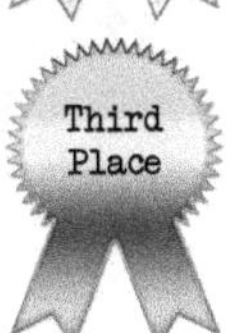

The Fish Tie, Mom, and Transference
Johnnye Gerhardt

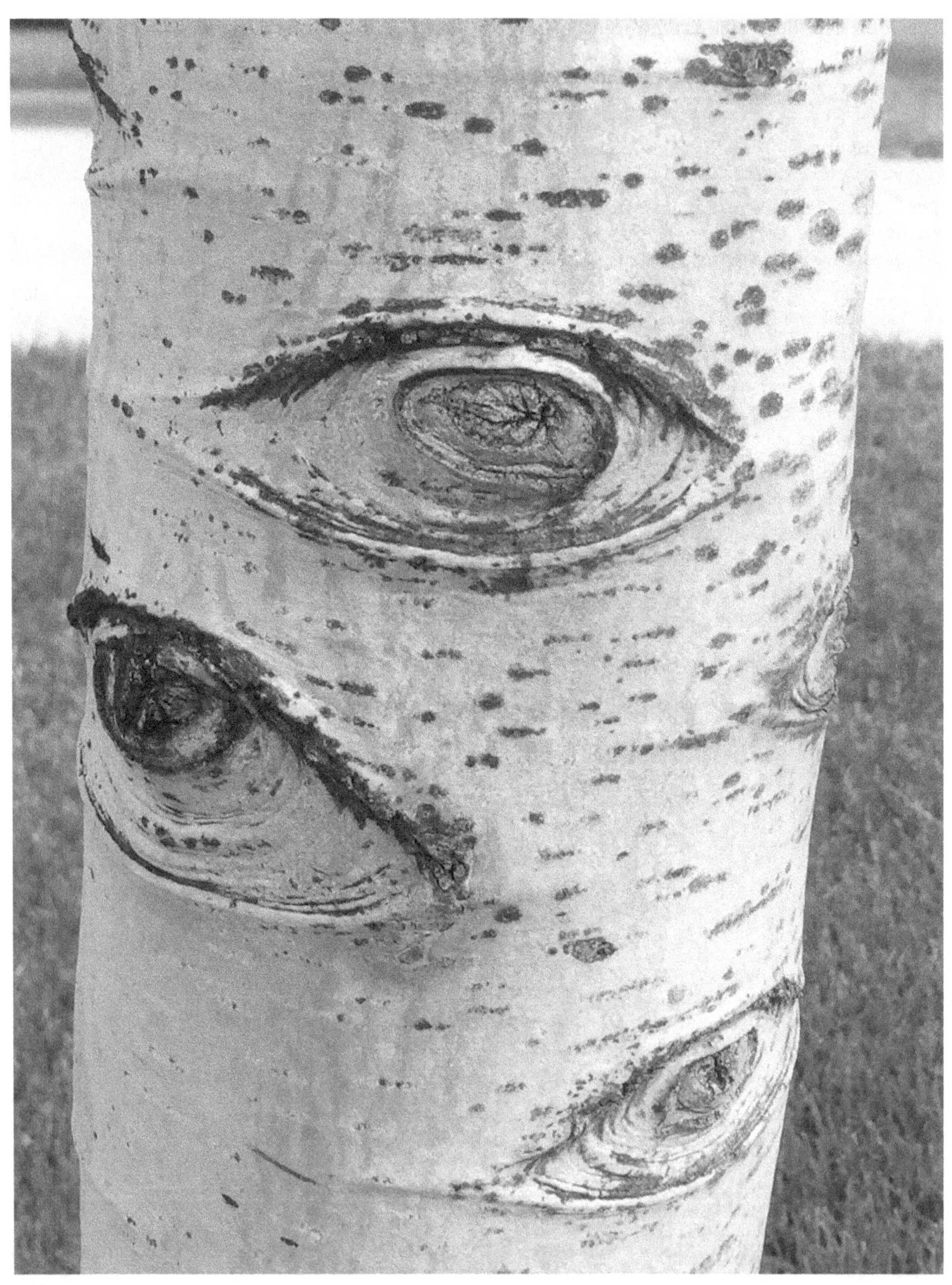

Introduction

Hey, is anybody out there? You. Yes, you people who thought Nebraska was just a flyover state with cattle and corn. We do have cattle and corn, but we also have a herd of creative people, and this book is a curated collection of curious tales and art.

If you're squeamish, then cover your eyes, because Nebraska authors are not shy about using the B word, the F word, the C word and every other alphabet word known to Mr. Webster (and some that might make him blush).

You'll read from the new as well as the notable, from teenagers through octogenarians, and from those with traditional values alongside others who are ushering in a cultural renaissance. You'll find words and work from artists living in the Big O on the east side of the state (Omaha), westward ho through the state capital in Lincoln where the penis of the plains atop the capitol proudly sows the heritage that founded this sod-busting land 150 years ago, to the western side of the state with its majestic sandhills and foothills before Colorado takes over.

So what's the big deal and why this book? The idea for this collection of mischievousness was stirred by the state of Nebraska's sesquicentennial celebrated in 2017. Our hope is that this anthology will go beyond a story of Nebraska as a state and become more of a state of mind. It's a voyeuristic peek into the hearts and minds of our Nebraska friends, neighbors, coworkers, and family members, and you are invited to join them on their path through life.

The idea behind *Misbehaving Nebraskans* was to find what is real. Not everything in this book is comfortable. Not everything is PG-rated. Not everything is R-rated either. Life can be messy sometimes, and complex issues and thoughts push their way into people's lives. How people deal with life is what we found most compelling among these stories.

Early in 2017, we sent out the call for submissions on today's version of the telephone party line: social media. We became the buzz in writers' groups and among anyone and everyone who could turn a word or create visual art. We expected "some" submissions (and hoped to have enough to publish a hefty book) and ended up receiving a tsunami of submissions. It was clear early on that making the final selections was going to be difficult. The process was demanding and took months beyond what we planned for.

If you're wondering how we then separated naughty from nice and decided which submissions to include in this book, please know that each submission went to a panel that graded and sorted the pieces with the goal of blasting the mountain down to a mere giant hill to send through semi-final judging. We trimmed to 300, then whittled again to 150. Even though the judging was a blind process, we set stringent measures to ensure that a wide variety of experience levels, topics, ages, and styles were included. Our goal for production purposes was to have about 100 pieces in the book, and we met that goal.

Our team compiled this book—a saga for the ages—that will inspire and enlighten, shock and titillate, amuse and arouse. Our respect and gratitude for the immense talent and creativity in the submissions grew beyond what even we imagined it could.

What began as a glimmer of an idea to honor and promote an open sharing of ideas, thoughts, feelings, and our Nebraska way of life, grew into a stunning portrait of Nebraska life. Here it is—done, and we are thrilled to publish the fine work of our fellow Nebraskans.

Kick off your shoes, rest your feet on something your mom told you not to, and turn a page into Nebraska history.

Lisa K Pelto Rachel Moore Ellie Godwin

Lisa Pelto and the Concierge Marketing Team

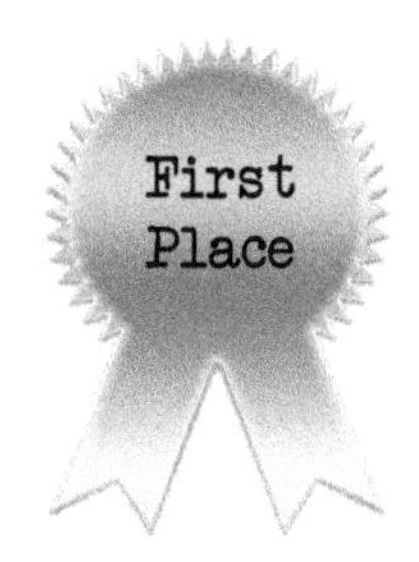

The Merry Widower

Robert Mundy

Dying was no fun, though, if I say so myself, I've adjusted rather well. But then I've always been a realist. And I was ready. Let me tell you, cancer gets old pretty quick. Two months may sound like no time at all to you, but it seemed like an eternity to me. Of course, now I know what an eternity really means.

It's not a walk in the park for the family, either. Truth be told, Bill was ready to have me go, though I could tell he felt guilty about it. I did what I could; telling him it was the natural way of things, like the seasons and all that. But he was always more guilt ridden than I was, more Catholic. I don't think non-Catholics understand the liberation of confession. Bill always said it was perfect for repeat offenders.

We were both freshmen in college when we met. It wasn't long before we had plenty to confess. By the end of the school year I was pregnant. A month later we were married, and by the end of the year Bill Jr. arrived. Sex with Bill was the first "going all the way" sex I'd ever had. He was also my last, though there was a fleeting extracurricular thought a time or two. As for Bill, I had my suspicions about his golf trips. No Tiger Woods syndrome, mind you, just a funny feeling I had. Now, all bets are off for me. As for Bill, well, sex is all he's thinking about these days. He's like a junior high boy who has discovered his magic wand. Not a pretty picture. Just for the record, I don't begrudge him the companionship—and the pleasures—of a relationship. But couldn't he have waited a decent interval?

You might be interested in knowing how I know all this. After all, sooner or later, you're going to wind up here yourself. Picture a bubble, transparent—that's a big word these days, transparent—flying through the friendly skies. Now imagine me as the air in the bubble. You can't see me, but I can see you, and I can read your thoughts or anyone else's I bring to mind. Last week I looked in on my high school boyfriend, and that was an eye-opener. It's also great for celebrity voyeurism. Or, I can close my eyes, relax, and let my mind go blank. Dead or alive, we all fill our time one way or the other.

I never would have guessed who Bill would take up with: Jan, from our gourmet dinner group. It started with a cherry pie, Bill's favorite. "Just being neighborly," she said as she roosted on our doorstep, pie in hand, her pretty face registering sympathy and concern. She wasn't the only one, but she was the most persistent. She hoped she could help him "get over the hump." She who had gone through the trauma of losing a mate when her husband, Ron, drunk as a loon, wrapped his car around a tree on his way home from a go-go joint. Soon, she and Bill were gabbing on the phone like a couple of giddy teenagers.

Now they're on their first big adventure, a weekend in New York City, flying first class, going to the opera. Bill and I always flew coach, even to Italy two years ago for our fortieth anniversary. We didn't care for the opera. Jan does. She's on the Opera Omaha board. Jan likes big, important boards. Bill and I preferred roll-up-your-sleeve-and-work-on-things boards.

It probably won't surprise you that this is the first time I've been to the Plaza. Bill and I always agreed there was no point in overpaying for a New York hotel when you spent so little time in the room. Now that I see the room, I see that we were right. Yes, it's larger, but a room's a room; countertop for phone and computer, coffee table in front of a small couch behind which the carpet is slightly frayed, nightstands with reading lamps on each side of the king-size bed.

Even with the weight Jan's gained over the last few years, she still thinks of herself as a beautiful woman. I have to admire her for that. It gets harder every year for a woman to feel that way. Of course, it helps when the lights are dim, like now. The thing about Jan is that she has style. Although she's never been subtle about her ambitions—the right country club, the right friends, the right organizations—when it comes to her appearance, she's tastefully understated. I hate to say it, but she's classy, and so far as I can see she hasn't had any plastic surgeries.

They are sitting side by side on the sofa. Bill is sniffing the air like a hunting dog, enraptured by her perfume. He puts his bad arm around her, the left one with the rotator cuff tear. They kiss, passionately, and they groan as if they're doing sit-ups. Bill is breathing heavily, and I wonder if Jan knows he's on blood pressure medication. Now they're up. Ouch! Bill took a rather nasty jolt to his shin when he bumped into the coffee table. He might have fallen down if he hadn't braced himself with a hand on Jan's ample hip. She is much stouter than I ever would have guessed. And Bill has gained a few pounds. Perhaps he's eaten too much cherry pie. They've reached the bed now, and they seem to be racing to shed their clothes and get under the covers.

Well, I'm glad that's over. All in all, it was actually rather tame. They are sitting up in bed now, table light on at low wattage, Jan with her head nestled on Bill's good shoulder. She asks Bill: "Does it make you feel, I don't know, funny, I mean wrong somehow that we've had sex, I mean, about Carol?" Of course I can read her thoughts, and she doesn't feel guilty. She's pleased as punch.

Bill looks down at her. "Not really," he says, but he has that hurt-little-boy look that men try to conceal, and he's thinking about a conversation we had a few months before we learned of my cancer, when death and dying was still an abstraction. "No," he continues, "Carol and I talked about this, you know, generally, that a surviving spouse should try to be happy."

Like a contented cat, Jan makes a murmuring sound, and she cradles Bill's left hand in her hands. Bill is picturing me in that old photo that he kept at his office, and I know it's time to go. It's not as easy as it sounds. Once I leave him, there's no coming back. There's a one-time, twenty-four-hour limit per person on voyeurism. Anything over that would be haunting, and that's forbidden up here. I like to think he'd do the same if he were watching me.

Death's Bad Hand

Marilyn June Coffey

When death comes
it's gonna come
like a bad hand
of solitaire
played on a computer
where you know better
but can't cheat
can't turn the pile
extract that empty
black King hidden under
the three of Hearts

can't turn a bum deal
into a win

Nope
all your wishes
all your wisdom
will be stacked up against
the intractable move
of a binary god
who doesn't give a damn
about your Jack of Spades fate

So eat your heart out
It's his deal

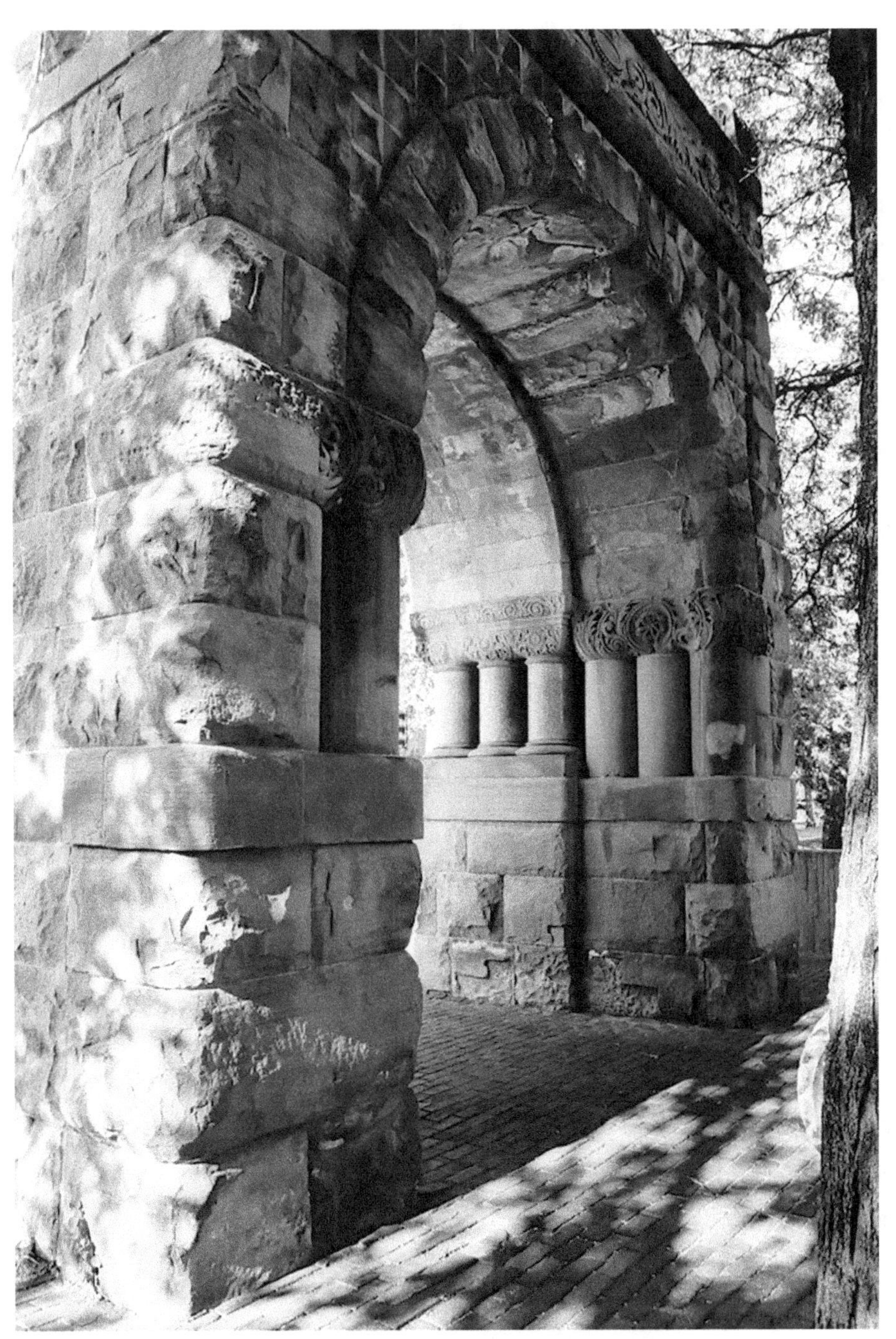

Central Park

Julian Adair

Poets have been mysteriously silent on the subject of cheese

Charlene Neely

Poets have been mysteriously silent on the subject of cheese
says G. K. Chesteron,

and yet most of us live
on a diet of bread and cheese –
muenster and provolone,
goat cheese and cottage cheese,
slabs of cheddar,
rounds of edam.

On days when a check
is found in our mail,
we glorify the cheese
with ground beef.

Days when the mail
doesn't come at all,
a bit of macaroni
will stretch it enough
to invite a fellow poet
to share our largesse.

And having licked the bowl
clean of the last remnants of cheese,
we will take up our pens

to write glorious odes
    to Grecian urns,
        to coy mistresses,
            to fallen heroes,
never mentioning the cheese.
The very sustenance of our lives.

Later, gathered in little cafes,
we eat salads with Feta cheese,
wash them down with cheap ale.
A tourist or two may happen by
to ask if we are famous
        (of course we lie!).
They ask if we'd mind smiling
for the cameras around their necks –

    maybe we should say
        String Cheese!

Star

Jeanne Batten Lynch

The cows usually came in from the pasture around milking time. They wanted their grain and they wanted to be rid of their milk. On this one night they were late so Daddy said, Sis, go see what's holding those cows up. They were a good quarter of a mile away, down in the corner of the pasture. As I approached them I saw that Star, our newest and youngest cow, was lying down. The other cows were standing there just looking at her. I was amazed at the placid look they had in their eyes. I had found the word "dumbfounded" in the dictionary before school closed for the summer but had never found a way to fit it into a conversation. This was it—the cows were dumbfounded.

I could hear Star softly moaning. She was lying on her side, with one hind leg up in the air. Her belly was going up and down and her eyes were very wide open and scared. I stepped closer and saw what looked like blood oozing out of her butt. I froze, and then it slowly dawned on me that maybe she was going to have a calf.

Whatever was wrong didn't matter; she needed help badly and for some crazy reason I also thought she needed privacy. I turned around and screamed at the cows; I ran at them and threw some clods of dirt, hitting one right on the tail. They started to run. Their bags flopped back and forth and I couldn't help but think they could use bras. Daddy was watching and he started to run toward us, yelling at me to "Stop chasing the cows!"

By now I could hardly breathe and tears were coming to my eyes. I got the message out that Star was lying down and bleeding. Daddy started to run, passing me. I tried to follow him but could not keep up. Then he was yelling, "Go get Mama, have her bring the car, tell her Star needs help."

I ran to the house and stammered out my message. A pot of potatoes boiled wildly on the stove. Mama ran toward the car, calling back, "Go to the horse barn and get a halter and a blanket, but first open the corral gate to let me through and then lock it good so the cows won't get out."

Tommy did not know what to do. Blaine started to cry. Grandma said, "Tommy, wiggle the buggy and shut Blaine up." Our dog, Trixie, started barking and running in circles. After I closed the corral gate, I caught Trixie and locked her in the horse barn. I knew she was the last thing we needed to deal with now.

I found a halter and a fairly clean horse blanket and ran across the field in Mama's tracks. Mama was driving really fast; I watched the car skitter and swerve in the deep alfalfa. I had to stop—my lungs were screaming and my heart was jumping. By the time I reached Star, there was a baby calf on the ground beside her and Daddy was rubbing it hard, and Mama was patting Star and saying, "Good girl, good girl." I knew that the halter needed to go on Star so I put it on her very gently. I handed Mama the blanket and she and Daddy slid it under the calf and then very carefully loaded it into the trunk. When she saw her calf go into the car, Star started to try to get up. Mama pulled the halter rope and Daddy lifted her back end. She stood for a minute and then wobbled toward the car. I climbed in beside Mama and we drove very slowly as Daddy led Star. She was determined to keep an eye on her baby.

Mama pulled up as close as she could to the horse barn. I opened the door and Trixie shot out which was okay now. I couldn't believe it when Daddy handed me the halter rope. I had to scramble out of Star's way as she staggered into the stall. She was breathing heavily.

Mama and Daddy carried the calf in and got it to stand up beside her and they pushed one of her tits into its mouth. Daddy held the calf up while Mama ran to the tank and brought back a bucket of water for Star. When I looked up, there was Grandma and Tommy with Blaine in the buggy. Grandma said it was a nice-looking calf. Daddy smiled and said, "It's thanks to Sis that it's alive." Then he whispered to me, "You have your answer now. This was calf birth. Childbirth is about the same."

How did Daddy know I wanted to know how babies get here? Did he know my thoughts? He probably knew a lot of them, like how much I hated the mean old priest. And he probably knew I was fighting the concept of sin as far as it applied to me. Daddy and I were close even though he didn't talk much. He paid attention to me. We didn't have a big dictionary at home so I often asked him the meaning of words or why some things happened and how things worked. He knew I eavesdropped when Mama's friends talked.

I looked around at my family. We were all marveling at how the little calf was already standing and gulping down milk. Mama was holding Blaine, and the rule that your hands should be clean when you touched him no longer seemed to be the case.

My mind slipped back to what Daddy had said before he whispered the word "childbirth." He had said it was thanks to me that the calf was alive. That filled me with spinning emotions. But before I completely wrapped myself in that pride, I said, "It was her friends, the cows who really saved her. If they had left her alone, we might not have noticed she was missing for a while." They looked dumbfounded but they weren't dumb. But they weren't overly smart either. Not one of them had run ahead and looked for Daddy like Trixie would have done—like I did.

Then Daddy turned to Mama and said, "Isn't there some kind of saying that if you save a life then you own that life?" In most things Mama was way smarter and quicker than Daddy. When she graduated from high school she even had a certificate to teach school. But it was during the depression, and men got all the jobs because they probably had a family to feed; so Mama never got to earn a real pay check. She knew right away what Daddy was referring to. She didn't go into it because she could see Daddy wanted to go on with his idea.

Daddy said to me, "I'm not saying that you can own this little calf. It's not going to be yours to sell or anything like that, but it can be yours to take care of if you like."

"What?" Grandma butted right in, "What's wrong with you? She doesn't know anything about caring for a calf." Daddy looked right at her and said, "Sis knows a whole lot more about a lot of things than you credit her for. Between her and Star, this calf will do fine. Star will trust her and that's what counts."

Grandma turned with just enough anger to help hoist herself up over the threshold of the barn door, and back into the yard she went. Mama asked if she would like to ride back to the house in the car. She paused a minute and then plopped herself in the passenger seat. Mama handed her the baby and off they went.

Daddy said to Tommy, "We need to let the cows into the barn and get them fed. Sis, you stay here and just watch that Star is okay. Tell me right away if she starts bleeding again from down there."

I felt almost dizzy; I dug into my brain to look for a good word to explain my condition. I knew I was over excited. The perfect word—overwrought—didn't come forward until I lay in bed that night sorting through the day.

Daddy and Tommy came back and the three of us just stood there in silence looking at Star and her baby. Finally, I asked, "Is it a boy or a girl?" Daddy didn't know either, and in all the excitement he hadn't looked. He ran his hand along the calf's belly and said, "Guess she's a girl, she doesn't have the boy thing." Tommy started to giggle.

Daddy said, "We should go eat, let the cows relax a little more. You sure got them to running, Sis." Then he turned to Tommy and said, "Ordinarily it's not a good thing to make cows run, gets their milk all stirred up. We don't want them making butter." Tommy laughed, he got the joke. Daddy was talking straight at him, like he was older.

We scrubbed our hands and arms hard with the lye soap Mama made. It burned a little which meant it was killing the germs.

Mama rushed around in the kitchen. She was making gravy from the roast juice and slicing bread. The potatoes burned when Grandma had decided to go to the barn to see what was going on and left them boiling on the stove. She had gotten the peas shelled and they were in the pot. I brought the big bowl of lettuce, tomatoes and radishes to the table from beside the sink. Then I got the milk out and Tommy looked over the table to be sure we had everything we needed there. And Blaine, bless his little heart, was busy in the buggy dumbfounded at his hands.

We rushed though supper as we were running almost two hours late. A predator could have slipped into the chicken house and killed them all by now. The cows were really getting uncomfortable. Some of them were complaining by letting out loud bawls.

Our usual routine was that Daddy, Mama, and Tommy went outdoors to do the chores after supper and I stayed in the house with Grandma and we washed the dishes. Then I folded clothes or played with Blaine.

Tonight, I led the way back to the horse barn. Daddy and Tommy followed me in. Star was asleep with the baby snuggled up close to her. We smiled at each other and Daddy said to me, "Go get three or four inches off the hay bale in back, put in it in the manger for Star. Do it quiet, don't wake her up. I'll send Tommy back with a can of oats for her to eat in the morning. I'll bring her some more water when we get done milking."

I lingered there for just a few more minutes and then headed back toward the house to get started on the dishes. I could hear Blaine screaming. I ran into the house. The dishes were all still on the table. Grandma had just gone to her room and shut the door and left Blaine there alone to scream.

His neck was nice and strong now so I could pick him up and carry him around without supervision. He was a dear sweet easy little boy until he got mad, and then he could temper like a crazy person. He was roaring mad now and probably scared. Even he knew you just don't walk out on a baby and close the door.

I brought him to Grandma's rocking chair and cuddled him and talked to him gently even though I was as raging mad as he was. Mama came rushing in the door. She looked around and said, "Where's Grandma?"

I just nodded my head toward her door. Mama grabbed Blaine up, and practically sat on me as I struggled to get out of her way. She ripped open her dress and pushed him on, took a big sigh and slowly started to rock him. I didn't look at her but did notice that pretty soon she buttoned her dress around him.

As I scraped the plates and stacked them, I blurted, "Why is Grandma so mean?"

Mama hesitated a minute and then she said, "You mustn't say that, Jeanne. Grandma's not mean. Her knees bother her." I thought, to myself, *so what, I'll bet her knees hurt just as much in her room as they do out here.*

I slept fitfully that night. I was, after all, "overwrought." My lungs still hurt and my legs were feeling funny, tight like they were going into knots. I began to think that maybe adults were right about hiding childbirth from kids. I would not have wanted to see Mama bleeding like Star was, although I could have been clued in on the fact that a baby was coming.

I woke up early and slipped out of the house, it was just dawn and the air was damp and chilly. There were a few twinkling stars still hanging there in the gray of the sky. Yes, Twinkle, was the perfect name for the calf.

Star was standing up eating the hay I had left her. I patted Star as I talked to her. Daddy had warned us to be very quiet and watchful around new mother animals. If they thought you were going to hurt their babies, they would take you on and hurt you. He was very stern when he talked about mother pigs. They would never give you the benefit of the doubt. In fact, he forbade Tommy and me to ever go into the pig pen.

Later during breakfast, Tommy said, "What are you going to name her?"

I said, "Twinkle." Tommy giggled and started to sing "Twinkle, Twinkle, Little Star" very softly. I hadn't thought of that!

Then I told him about the fit Blaine threw last night, not that he didn't have reason. We laughed. For such a little baby he could really get mad. We were never rude enough to laugh at him to his face when he went off for no apparent reason. But sometimes we did sneak off and laugh after Mama settled him down.

The minute Grandma laid down her spoon from stirring her morning coffee, I grabbed it, used it to scrap the breakfast plates into the animal food bucket and then snapped the dirty dishes into the sink. I was getting good at making my point. If she didn't want to help with the dishes, that was fine with me. I scrubbed them quickly, stacked them in the dish rack, and covered them with a towel.

Grandma got up and went back to her room.

Another Thing I Would Not Tell My Mother

Heidi Hermanson

Me and the pastor's son—Josh—
drank grape kool-aid
and vodka one summer
til we passed out on the riverbank.
A true friend, he held
my head while I regurgitated
in various shades of violet. Later, my hand.
He was angling, all right,
but I wasn't a fish
to be caught and he knew it.
We had been there since before sunset
picking out smooth stones,
tonguing names of small towns:
Nodaway, Clarinda, Nishnabotna -
The cottonwood
sent the breeze through
us like magic. Our faces painted
with excitement, we shed
our clothes and danced
like hooligans before jumping
in, sliding under the cool
water of time. In the distance
a dog barked, regular with rhythm.
It's that old dog of dawn
that reminds us why we do
everything, stripping down
in front of Time
to reveal who we really are.

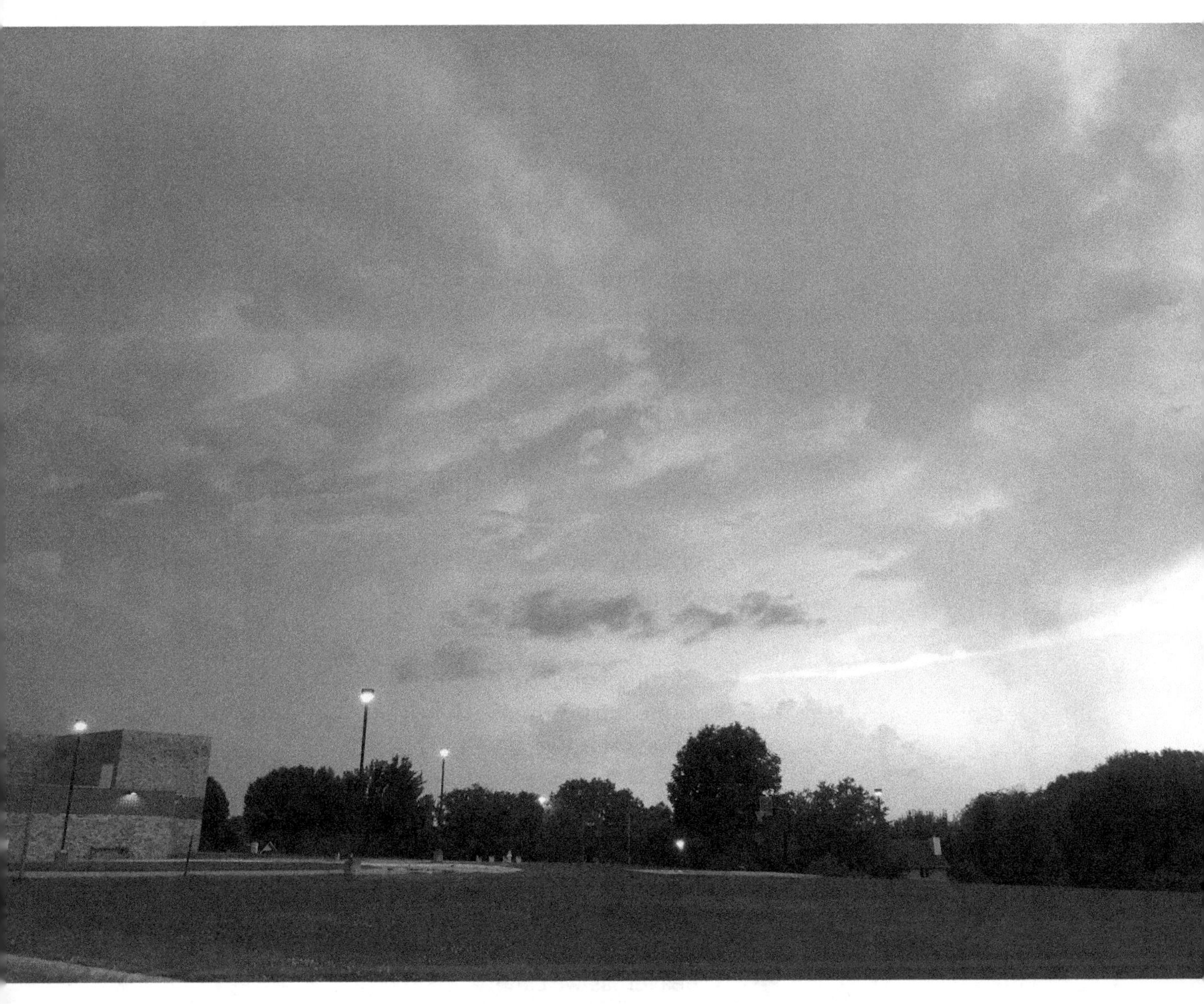

Stormy

Ellie Godwin

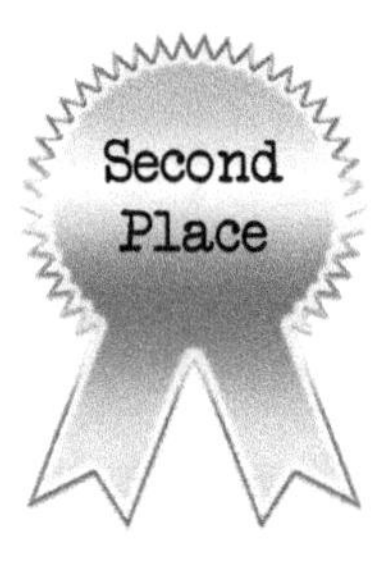

The Provocateur

Marilyn June Coffey

i

Here I live
in a town whose city dads decreed
a bare body, glimpsed though a window
against the law

Here they punish not he who glimpses
but she who bares the body
except in those rare cases
when baring a body in one's own home
might be justified:

say a matron rises naked
unexpectedly from bed
to dash to the phone
receive the news her pere
at 93 has 'passed away'
as we put it out here

say her bare body
is momentarily glimpsed
that's not illegal

as long as it's not 'provocative'
explained the fathers

changing my definition of the term
from a woman spraddle-legged
on her porch swing, baring
'beaver' as we call it
or leaning out an open window
bare breasts supported by the sill
crooking a finger: 'psssst!'

to myself,
trekking naked to the frig at 3 a.m.
suddenly again, after all these years
provocative
to him who glimpses me bare
momentarily illuminated
by my night light.

ii

I recall with longing my early naked
childhood freedom so soon gone
remember my adolescent gazing
at *National Geographic* spreads
where nubile girls grind grain in public
pert nipples pointing horizonward
where mothers nurse unabashedly
& grand dames swing their dual sacks
hung flat as empty pillow cases
How I marveled at a life with no 'hurry up
get dressed, Daddy's coming up the walk'
Papa presumably unable to control himself
so I must do it for him.

iii

Can't help but wonder
watching my male neighbor
catch the morning breeze
on his bare torso
as he mows the lawn
can't help but wonder if
after next Friday when I rise
one-breasted from the surgeon's saw
the other but a tuck & scar
can't help but wonder if our
city fathers will find it
provocative
should I then strip to my waist
mow my lawn.

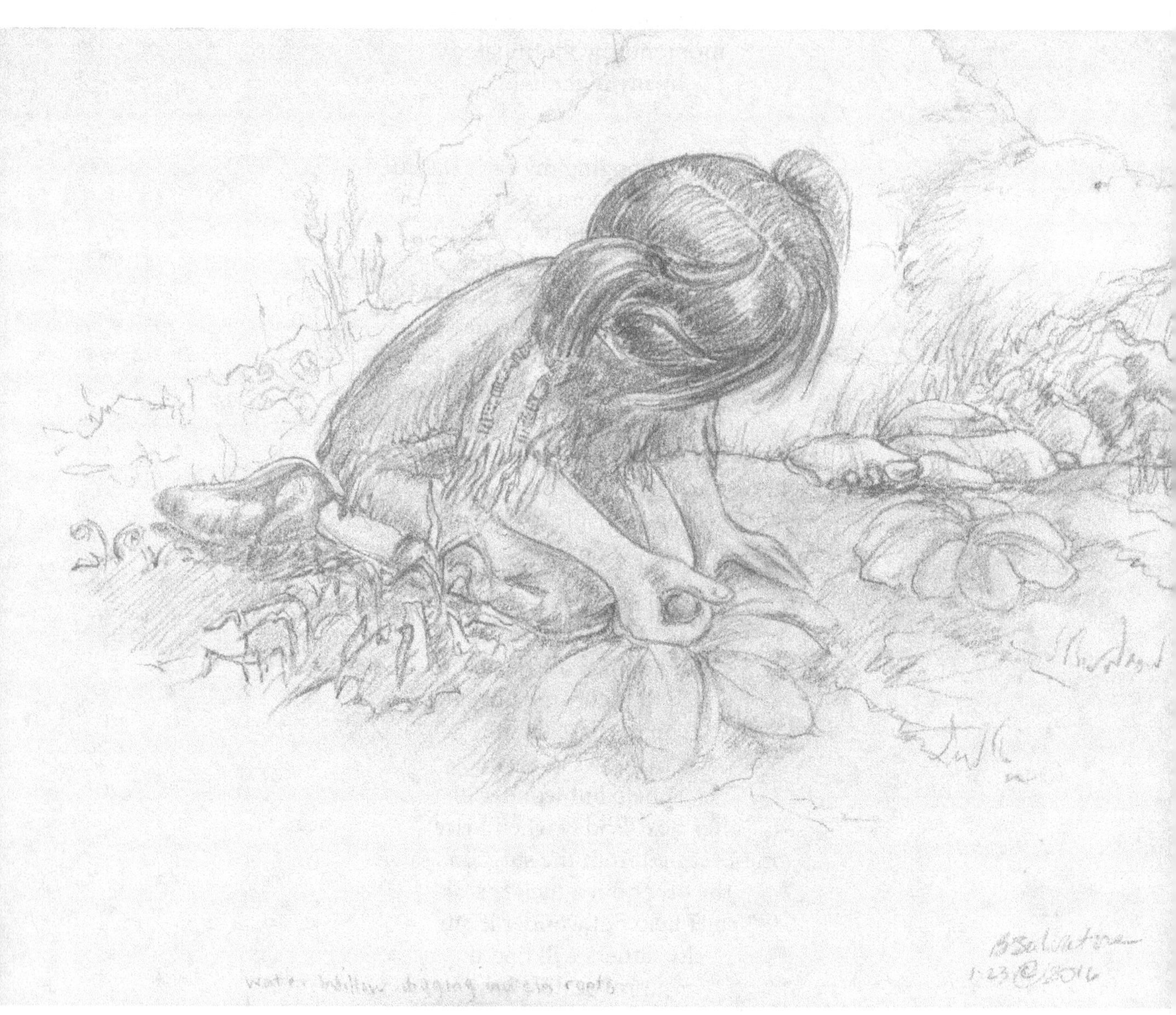

Bear Root Digger

Barbara Salvatore

Night Court

Rhonda Rieck-Rush

Moon adjourns
black silk sky disrobes
to daybreak

Old Barn

Rhonda Rieck-Rush

Old transparent barn
sway slightly
with spring's shifting breeze

Faces

Barbara Salvatore

I see faces everywhere
I see faces in the wood grain
in the folds of that towel
in linoleum swirls and stucco ceilings
I see faces from years of staring, at that ceiling
as a child, wishing, they would scream and shout
but they were helpless, as me
under him
Frozen there in plaster
faces with wispy outlines, half open mouths.
Remember That, one with round sockets instead of eyes
a bun high up on her head.
I see faces figures animals running in the coals of a fire
Smoke and clouds turn to dragons
Raccoons and ducks, fly small across the sky
In clouds, I see things other people may not.
I notice shadows and how they make a person a superhero
at just the right time of day
long legs broad shoulders strong hips giant fists.
The faces do not scare me, in the ceiling
in the shadows, everywhere
an everyday reminder
that I am not alone
never helpless, not abandoned
never alone.
Even then.
Never alone

Voices.
Something smarter yelling
Run Run Run!
Away.
I look up.
Faces in stars and clouds
in the walls around me
bathroom tiles
wood grain, marble, mirrored glass
Reflections of other people, shadow ghosts
spirits lingering, spirits helping, me
Ancestors, allies, angels
animals, ghosts, dragons
All, right here by my side

Faces
I have always known
I am never alone.

Wayward Wishes

Max R.A. Thomas

I searched between the sands
For the Promised Lands
But doubt devours
In between idle hours
For what I seek I haven't the faintest notion.

My anxieties whisper;
As my heart's desires drastically differ
I wonder if my hopes and dreams were just copy/pasted
And I begin to add up all this time I've wasted
Making lots of movements, but with no motion.

In indecision I stand still as a post,
Enraged with myself for letting me become this shell, this ghost.
No matter what I choose, I'll never be a winner
For I have done nothing to justify my life as a sinner,
Nothing but small displays of compassion to catch my descent.

I dream covetously of glorious grandeur
But no love I have been shown has given my dissatisfaction cure.
All the things I have said in jest
No one could have cleverly guessed
Were uttered to mask my malcontented heart's lament.

On my soul grows pastures of asphodels
As I keep my true self walled like a citadel
'Til I confuse her with the public's decoy.
Their persons differ, but so does the usage of their employ;
This is the factor that causes me to forget.

One of these days, and I fear it coming soon,
My life will reach dusk and my spirit will rise as the moon.
She will sing truth once silenced by her prison
And the uniform stars will be forced to finally listen.
Perhaps only then I will make peace with my regret.

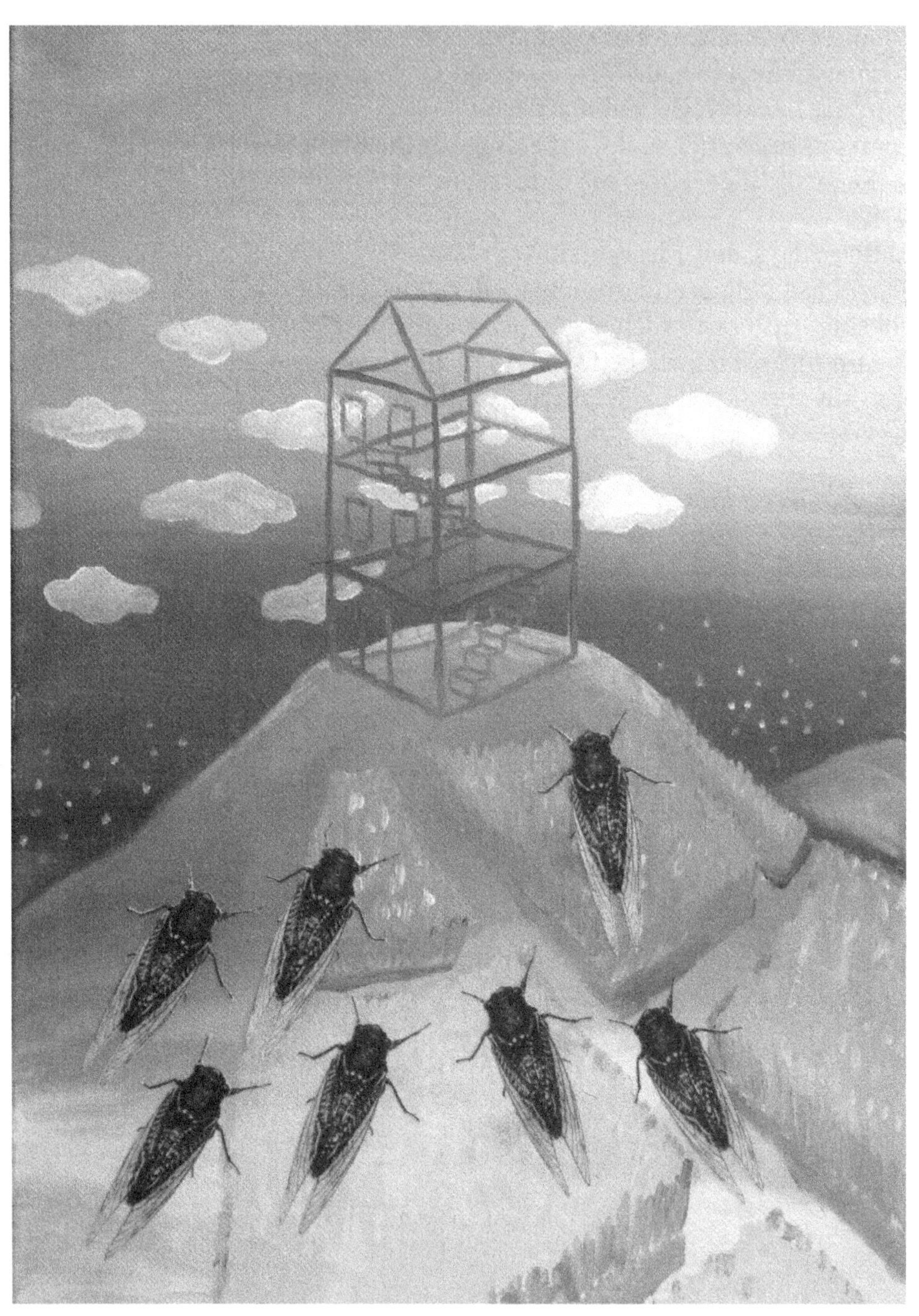

cicadas outside

Joe Pankowski

I Needed a Break

Gaylene Quinn

THE OBSERVER

I can say what drew my attention to this woman, a prisoner of the state
A beauty, so confident, she didn't belong
It was hard to believe she committed a wrong
"There's been a terrible mistake" she spoke plainly, without malice or hate
"A quick swerve to the left and my life would be saved"

THE TRUCKER

The car's right tires miss my head by a few, mere, inches
As I lay beside the yellow line
The asphalt feels cool and so fine
My body hangs low, knees scraping, legs crawling, jaw clenching
Drunk and injured my only thought, I want to find home

I remember crashing my truck through the field's barbwire fence
The speed, the momentum
Carried us and sent him
Flying, landing in the newly harvested cornfield, eyes wide, body tense
We separated, choosing two different paths

I remember the panicked passengers scrambling out of the car
Like ants fed poison
Down their hole, no survivors, none
"Find my friend" I beg them, my drinking buddy, a fixture at the bar
Is that him walking toward the distant cottonwoods
One person remained, fastened in the driver's seat, a night of fun turned wrong
Shell shocked at the turn of events
Her car with no sign of damage or dents
Just a few minutes earlier laughing with her girls, belting out an oldies song
A little off key, a lot distracted

I think about my girlfriend, the one on speed dial, not my booty call
Will she cry at the funeral?
Grief shared, at times communal
"There's been a terrible mistake" she spoke plainly, not able to stand at all
"A quick swerve to the left and his life would be saved"

THE DRIVER

In my defense, a disoriented person in the middle of a dark road
On a pitch-black night
Who would expect that kind of fright
Not to be spotted until the approach and then too late, a penance owed
"In my defense"—cheap words that matter nothing

His body broken, chest compressed, did I hit a speed bump
Breathe, slow down, rest
My body frozen, needing to be caressed
I hear the canine unit's dog bark, picking up the scent, jump
Forward, strain forward, pull on its leash.

My family sat through tortuous days of testimony, unsettled by what they heard
Excessive blood alcohol levels
Each fought their own wretched devils
The jurors stayed emotionless, attentive, as witnesses spoke word after word
At times I felt like we were both on trial
The foreman stood to read the verdict…my heart, like a horse gallops away
This recurring dream left fears anew
Haunt my daylight wanderings too
At the sight of my lifelong friends these thoughts I try to keep at bay
Rush in, like water waiting to fill an abandoned well
Prison could've been my fate but a quick swerve to the left saved his life, my life
Not one more mistake for my kids to endure
Not one less parent as they grow and mature
One more person to walk this earth, live out his purpose, perhaps take a wife
Second chances, innocence remembered

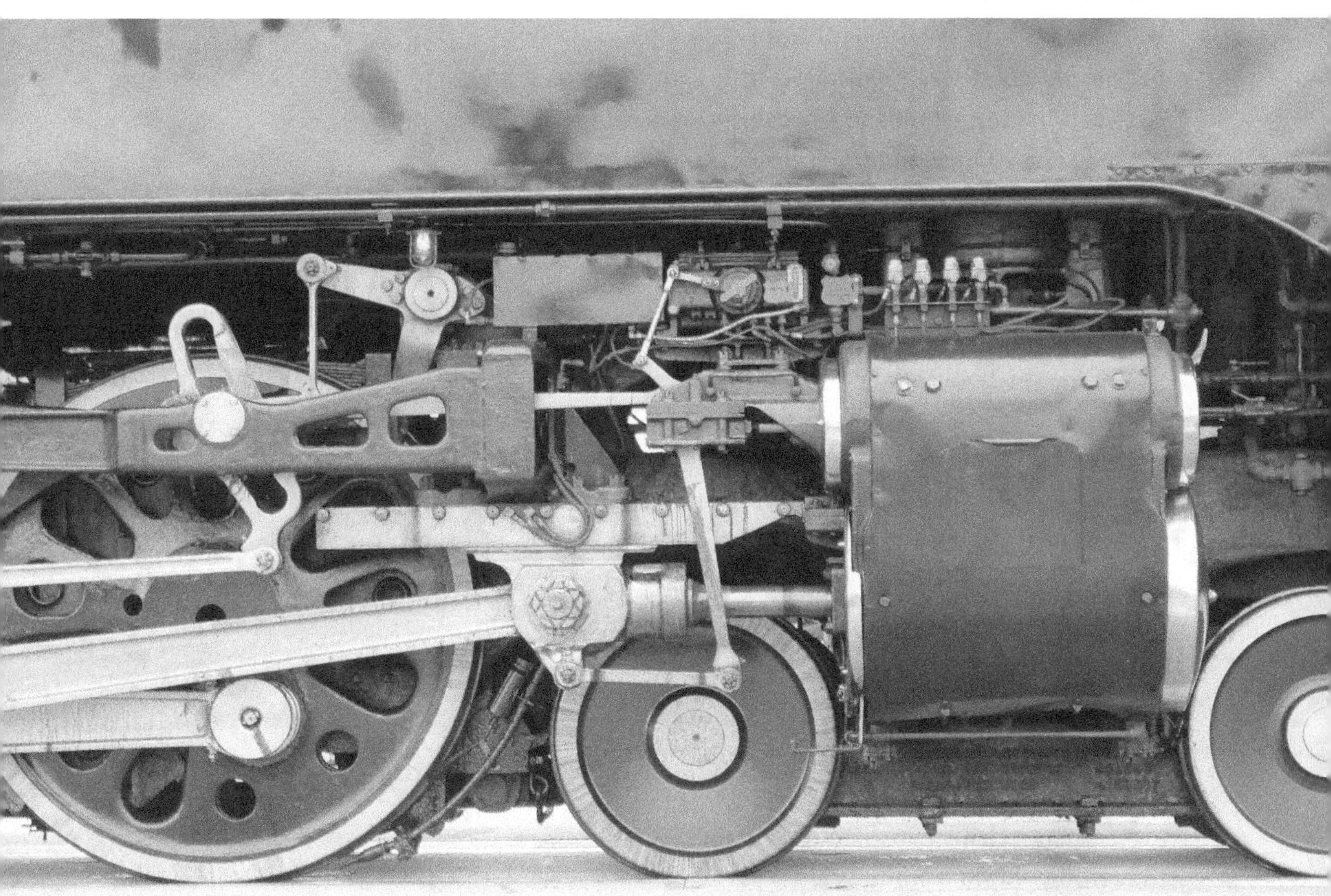

Close Up of 844

Chris Richter

Bittersweet Harvest

Terry Lee Schifferns

Outside my cabin birdsong flirts
with the distant, yet constant hum
of busy interstate semis almost a mile away.
Between the interstate and my cabin
a tamed river I love no longer flows
a mile wide, though sometimes a foot deep.
Beside this river, orange globes
of bittersweet burst from their
hard shells in late autumn—a flash
of brightness against drab khaki browns.

This river is dammed by those
who have never floated in her gentle embrace
and who wick her away to comfort
crops that do not belong
on these dry prairie plains—
crops that fatten cattle
that fatten already overfed,
well-bred zealots of over consumption
who do not recognize harm
even when it drips conspicuously from
the corners of their mouths.
They simply wipe it politely
away with a clean napkin
and smile guilelessly.

The bittersweet that blooms
rampant behind my cabin,
beside this river is a climbing
woody vine that is often gathered
as an ornamental plant—
Nature perfectly preserved and arranged
in Martha Stewart wreaths
to be hung and admired in lovely
suburban homes everywhere.

Some days I don't even notice the sound
but today the thrum of the distant semis
plows through me like the drumming
at a powwow—heart and soul and drum
all beating together…

I've come to accept the interstate noise
will always be here,
like I've come to accept the river
will always dwindle to a trickle each July,
like I've come to accept the dozers
will always move closer and closer,
like I've come to accept that there
will always be those whom I love who I
will never again see, at least,
not on this spinning marble.

All the same, today the interstate's
humming and the bird's singing
sounds like a harmony of sorts to me.

The Mayor of the Bottoms

Victoria Goessling

I do need to thank you, Detective Ferguson, I really do. I appreciate your taking the time to talk to an old woman like me. I know how busy you all are, and it just warms my heart that you always find the time to talk with me, even if it can only be for a few minutes.

Tea, you say? Why, yes, I guess that after all of our visits you do know that I like my tea. You're such a nice young man. I just wish that we'd met under better circumstances. I just wanted to touch base with you about my granddaughter Debbie's case.

Oh, I understand how hard it is to get people to talk to the police, I certainly do. It's a thankless job that you have sometimes. It must be so frustrating, asking and asking and getting no answers. My, this tea is nice. One sugar, just as I like it. Thank you again.

Do you know that I have always lived in a five-block area of where I am now? Except for when we got chased out by the flooding back in the fifties, of course. The river almost came to where my little house is now. That's why they call our little spot of heaven the Bottoms. Of course, an experienced officer such as yourself probably knew that. You probably know all the neighborhoods in this city.

Anyway, I was born just a block away from where I live, went to school two blocks away and never really wanted to live anywhere else, even if it is a tired old neighborhood. Lots of people look down on us there, you know, but that's just because they're ignorant. Mostly we just get ignored. Some people don't even know the area exists. Not as a place where people live, that is. All they see is the airport and the water plant and the factories and they don't think that real people live there. Funny how that is. The city even ignores us.

Oh, I don't mean you, Detective Ferguson, of course I don't. Please don't be offended. I mean the bigwigs, the city planners and such. They've forgotten us for all of my years, and that's why we have such crummy streets and not much lighting. Most of our streets don't even have signs. We hardly ever get plowed out unless one of the drivers clearing the airport and factory roads feels sorry for us, and that happens a bit. Mostly we're all fine with it.

The people who live around me are fine with it, or they'd leave. Some do, but some of us enjoy living apart from the rest of the city. We take care of ourselves and mostly get along just fine. We even elect ourselves an unofficial mayor of the Bottoms, um hum. I've held that post for the last thirty-one years. We all cast our votes at Buddy's Place over on Fourth, you know where that is? Anyone sixteen and over can vote. We do it every presidential year.

What's that? Why do we let sixteen-year-olds vote? Well, why not? When the whole thing started back in the Depression, lots of people that age were already married and raising families, or joining the army and such. We've lost a lot of young people to wars, then the others come home and can't find jobs and we lose them to drugs and alcohol and other bad things, but we all stick together, yes, we do. I think the idea was if the young ones got a vote they'd see how important voting is. I know you're too young to remember, but there are people still living who remember when women and minorities weren't allowed to vote.

Minorities! Now that's a laugh, isn't it? Whoever decided that the good lord made white people the majority? Who did the counting? My mama always said that the value of a person is what's inside of him, not the covering. 'Don't you judge a book by its cover, LuAnne,' she'd say to me, and since she couldn't read, I guess she wasn't talking about books. The Bottoms never needed integration. We've always been so, and it's worked just fine, most of the time.

What does the mayor do, you ask? Well, lots of times it's just settling arguments between a couple of neighbors who can't afford lawyers and don't trust the police. I'm sorry to have to say that to you, because you've always been so nice to me and mine, especially with all of our troubles.

Anyway, sometimes there's a problem over dogs left out to bark all of the time or yards that grow waist high. Sure, the city handles that stuff, but lots of times a friendly chat with the mayor is good enough to settle things. Especially with my four big sons and now their boys, too. You wouldn't think a runt like me could have had such big sons, would you? Marvin was a big man and those boys take after him. Anyway, few people want to argue with a woman who has backup like that, and I'd like to say that most folks just plain like me and listen for that reason alone. I'd hate to think that it's being afraid.

My poor Debbie, well, she never used to be afraid and now she is. Of everything, after what those animals did to her. When I was her age I was already widowed and the best job that I could get was working in the cocktail lounge at the airport. I was a sassy little thing with all the right curves and lots of red hair. Mostly it was men traveling then and I'd toss that red hair and flash my big blue eyes and I made damn good tips every night. Then I'd walk home across that big ball field, through the rest of the park and the three more blocks home real late, usually two in the morning or so, and I'd be fine. If the weather was good and people were out, they'd all say hey. If the weather was bad I seemed to get to our little house faster, I'll tell you that. My cousin Raylene lived on my back porch for free and watched those boys of mine and life was pretty good. Raylene ended up marrying a worthless SOB and moving away, but after he beat her one time too many she came on back and stayed until she died last year.

Debbie's ma is dead, too, drunk driving like a fool, and her dad's in the VA home, so she lives in their little house 'round the corner from me. She got herself a job at the airport and when that old car of hers acts up, she walks the same way that I used to walk to get to and from work, but of course you know all that. It's in the reports.

I tell you, Detective Ferguson, she just breaks my heart nowadays. She was always so happy and bubbly. My little sunshine girl, that's what I'd call her. That sun done set for now, though, after all of her troubles.

I know that you know her car wouldn't start on that bad, bad night, so Debbie decided to walk on home. Damn thing died at the edge of the park and just wouldn't start up again. Tired as she was, Debbie figured that it'd be a quick walk home because the Bottoms is all flatland, you see. But I just want you to know that she's a good, hardworking girl, not some silly thing with no more sense than to walk through a park at night.

It's not like it was for me, oh, no. It most certainly is not.

You know that's where those animals grabbed her and I know you know what they did, the bastards. Did all of that and left her there, not caring if she was dead or alive. I hope they rot in hell.

Oh, yes, I know that you all are still looking for them, and I appreciate it. Problem is, sometimes people don't want to talk to the police. Sometimes they're afraid, sometimes they're hiding something, sometimes they don't know what they know, if you see what I mean.

Well, anyway, that nice Officer Hanson got me some of the, what-do-you-call-thems? Com-pos-ite sketches that your artist did from Debbie's description, and you know an old lady like me, well, I've got lots of time. Especially since Debbie got out of the hospital and is staying at her brother's. Not wanting to leave their spare room, she isn't. So, I started walking around that park and talking to everyone who hangs out there and you know how it is, no one's afraid of a little old lady and lots of them were downright nice to me, no matter how scary they looked. I'd ask and I'd ask and eventually someone knew a little something, then someone else and you must know how it goes.

I tried to tell the officer that I spoke to while you were on your vacation that I had nicknames and maybe even a real name, but he did not want to listen. What's that? There's nothing in the case notes about it? Well, I'm not surprised to hear it. He wasn't nice like you are.

Where was I? Oh, yes. After a while one of the nice boys in the park told me that he'd heard the animals were living in the no-tell motel over on Campbell Avenue, so I moseyed over there and sat on a bus bench for a couple of days and darned if it wasn't true. I knew them right away and they're in a room way at the back, living large and partying away.

Do you think that tattoos can ever be removed completely? That nice fellow who told me about the motel would be so handsome without that snake crawling up his neck, I think.

What rooms, you ask? And when did I last see them? Oh, it's the very last room on the east side, Detective Ferguson, and I saw them just before I came over here. You don't need to get excited. I expect they're still there. I certainly did my best to assure that, I promise.

How'd I do that? Well, you see, it's taken so long for the police to find them and then I hear all of the time about monsters like that getting off on a technicality that I made sure they wouldn't be raping anyone ever again. Let me show you something.

Oh, do calm down, Detective Ferguson. My Marvin taught me all about guns, he certainly did. This was his little Chief's Special. Hardly any kick, really, and easy to aim when you're real close.

They opened the door when I knocked, and I shot them where it matters. They should live to go to court, but if they don't, no harm. I'm old and close to dying anyway, so I really don't expect the court to be too hard on me. I'm a little old lady. Harmless. Even if they put me in a home full of crazies, that's okay. I'm tired of cleaning up my own house and one of the boys can have it. Probably could have asked the boys to take care of things, now that you mention it, but I didn't want to ask them to.

I am the mayor of the Bottoms and I do have responsibilities, I certainly do.

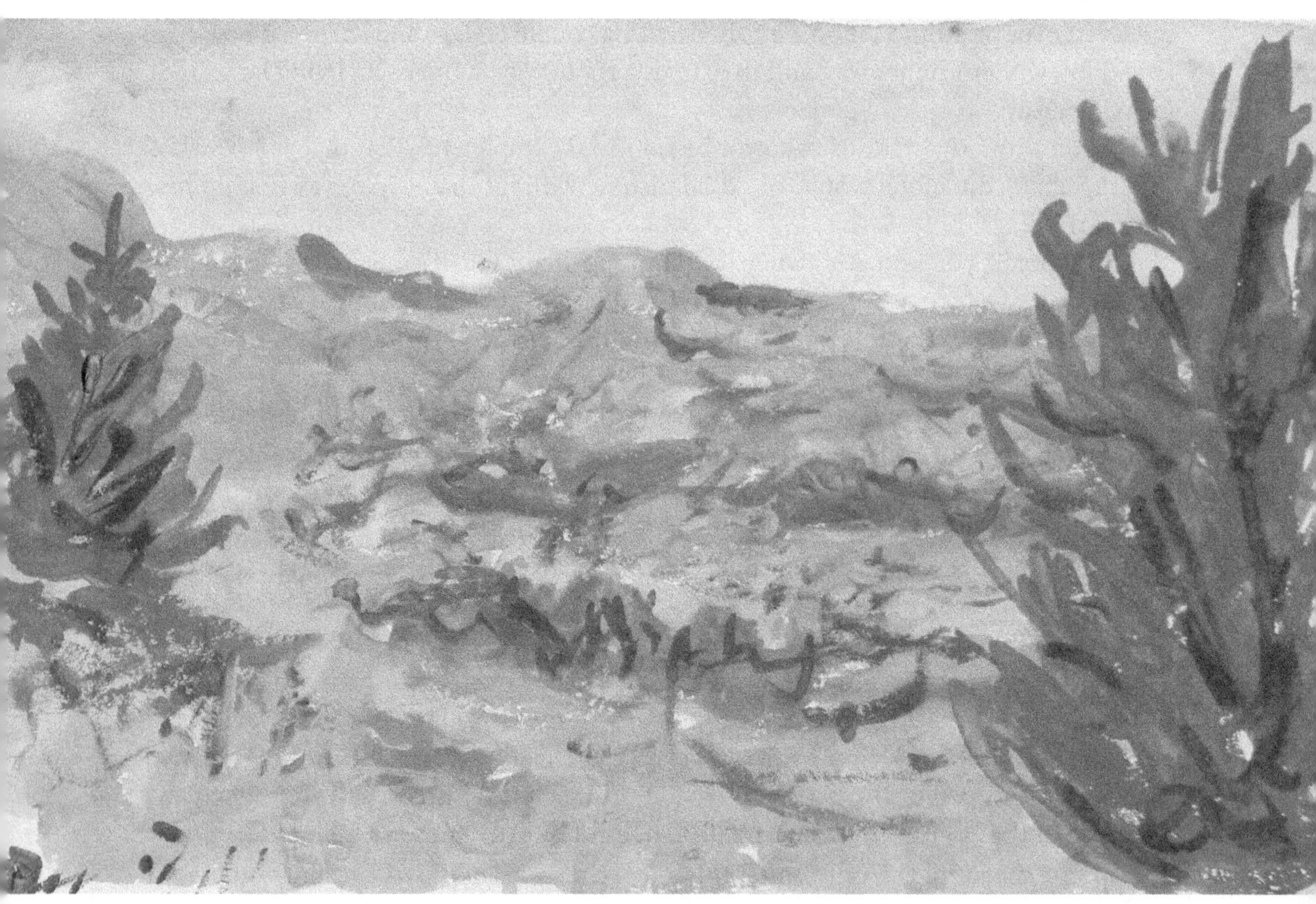

High Hills

Douglas Polk

Daffodils

Kaye de la Hulle

The daffodils are blooming
Beside the now abandoned house
Deep in the woods

How dare they flower
Now that she's no longer there
To admire their exquisite beauty.

To exclaim, oh, look George,
The daffodils are blooming!
Now it's officially Spring!

How rude of them, for after all
She, among all people, knew
How they foretold of life everlasting

So perhaps they rose from
The moist, fertile earth
To remind me, her daughter

That my mother lives on
Amid the delicate yellow blossoms
Scattered there beside the house.

Cottonwoods

Kathleen O'Brien

Tough
gnarled
with grey, deeply rutted bark,
their trunks grow fast and tall and thick,
then lean precariously.
Branches bend
like old men's backs.

Glory
is in their leaves—
leathery circles that come to the point
silver-green, then yellow-gold,
flashing sunlight,
always moving
creating music—
the percussion of
angels in a breeze.

In spring
seeds fly on white wings
and breezes plant them by waterways.

They thirst,
These natives of the plains,
And send out roots like soda straws.

As a child,
rumbling by in a wagon with her parents,
my grandmother
watched their grandmothers
sipping from the Platte.

The Druids worshipped trees.
Those ancestors of my ancestors
believed in trees
as I believe in Jesus.

If Druids had known the cottonwoods
as Grandma Ellen knew them
as I know them,
they might have built
a thousand shrines
along the Platte
and danced
in worship.

The leaves and cotton spirits
would have danced
with them.
Jesus and Ellen and I would have
danced with them.

The Dismal River

Kim McNealy Sosin

From deep clear wide constant
the aquifer waters bubble into sunlight
forming an icy blue pool.
We are all floating.

Subterranean, so much life,
water below, semi-arid land above
engraved by emerging twin rivulets
born in this underground gift.

North and South forks split valleys
once disputed by Sioux and Pawnee, now
cradle families on sun-kissed grasslands,
roots as deep as underground seas.

Dismal waters flow from rivers to oceans.
Teenagers on horseback ride into twilight.
Our waters, our tribes, our children, leaving.
Leaving us, Nebraska weeping.

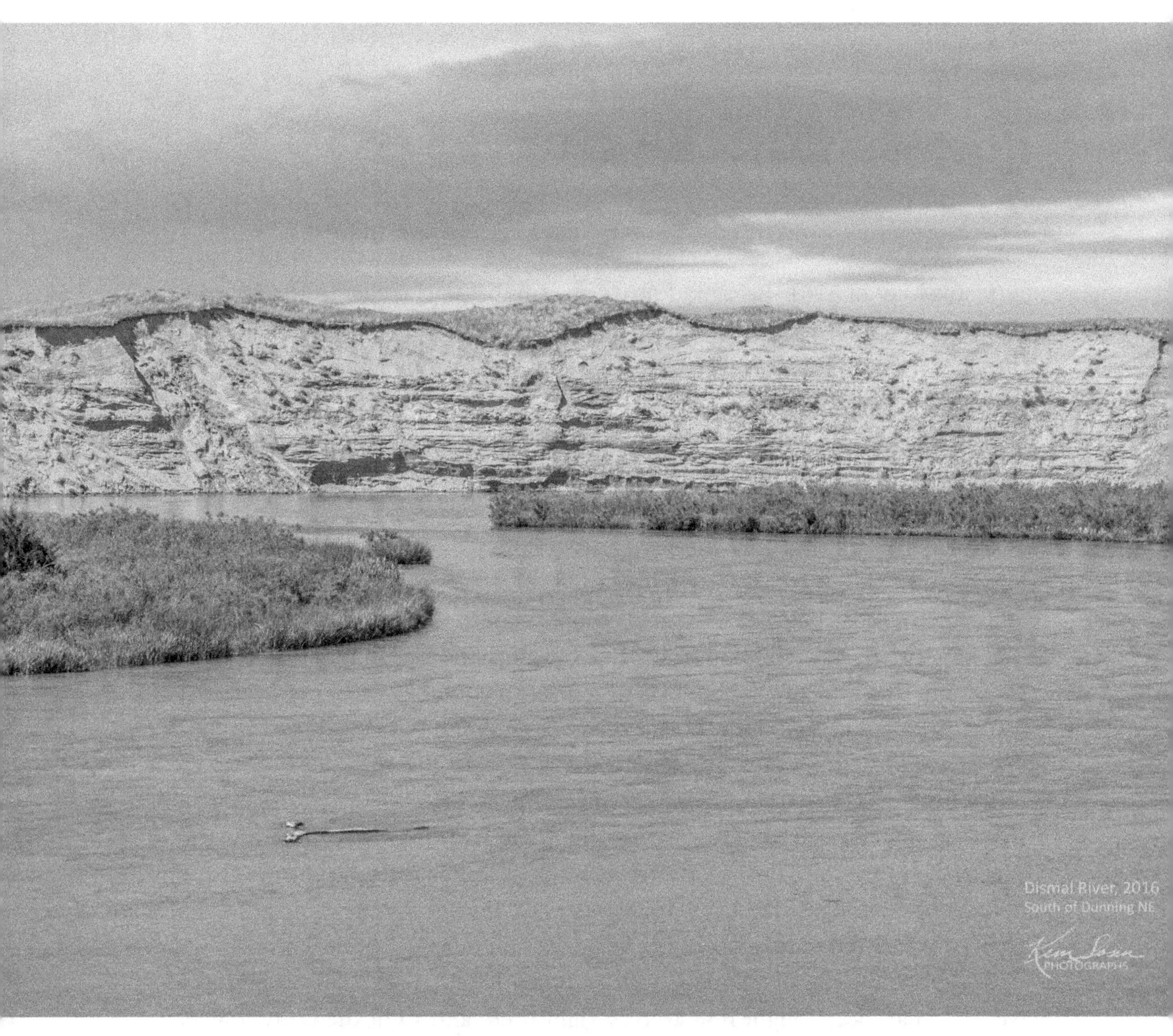

The Dismal River*

*A short "wild and scenic" river born in bubbling springs rising from the Ogallala Aquifer in the Sandhills of Nebraska.

Kim McNealy Sosin

The Making of Me

Marilyn Loy Every

It was May of 1961. Every kid in Custer County, Nebraska, in the 8th grade was there. Nearly every parent, grandparent and neighbor had crammed themselves into the wooden seats, side by side in that huge, hot sweaty tomb. I had reluctantly agreed with old Mrs. Mackey that it would be a good idea for me to play my best piano piece at that graduation ceremony. However, all I was thinking about in that moment was whether or not to run out through the musty red velvet drapery that separated me from the back door of the auditorium.

I looked down and saw the lovely pastel pink flowing down over my slightly budding breasts, cascading softly over my twelve-year-old narrow hips and thighs, and stopping just below my scuffed knobby knees. It was like an ocean of pink that comforted my trembling heart; like burying my face in a bunch of light pink carnations that were put in bouquets to comfort my mother when my Grandma died. I knew if my monkey mind didn't remember where to put my fingers on the piano keys, I would also be dead—just like my Grandma.

I was painfully shy. And, I knew it more so when my father tried to ridiculously shore up my courage to perform that night. He had instructed me to just look at everyone in the crowd as if they were a bunch of "cabbage heads." It sort of sounded like a good idea at breakfast that morning, but I did not see any cabbages as I briefly glanced across the audience looking for green and purple spherical heads.

Epilogue! Yes, it was Epilogue—that difficult and tricky Heller Etude Op.45 No.25—I had been taught how to play right there and right then. My fingers were spread widely as I buried them into the skirt of my dress. Cellular memory of the staccato beat pounded between my ears: *dah dah da dah dah…da dah dah da dah*! I felt my pupils grow wide. The light across the auditorium turned everything such a hazy white that I feared Jesus was coming.

My stomach began to roll and churn. It was as if I had just opened my tin lunch pail and the sickening waft of a minced ham sandwich crawled up my nose. It was actually worse than if ghosts of stark white Wonder Bread, old yellowish Miracle Whip and warm minced ham, with its slimy beads of oil, had all landed in the pit of my stomach. But, it was actually fear. Yes, it was a bolt of chilling fear that struck me, shot up my veins and paralyzed the synapses of my brain.

The spotlight high in the ceiling shone down on the old grand piano bench. The glaring reality was that the black bench was vacant. I wasn't sitting on it. The auditorium was silent… filled with a glut of anticipating eyeballs and heavy breathing emerging from the one giant lung. I gazed into the space of what seemed like a mile-wide stage, and latched my eyes on that leather bench with its scratched up, scrawny legs. My brain continued to fire one huge blast after another, spewing cortisol and adrenalin like wild rampant rivers during springtime storms. The reality of potential failure flooded over my willowy body, weakening my legs and cementing my new white high heel shoes right to the stage floor.

Then, as if I uttered a stammering "Yes" to Jesus, faith took me for a walk. With as much grace as I could muster, my high heels began to click across the wood floor. I made it to the piano and steadied my trembling hand on its tipped keyboard lid. Then, I turned and tucked my beautiful, flowy, pink skirt in front of the bench just behind my knees. A slow, deep exhale filled my ears, as I breathed in trust that my hands might know what to do when I couldn't consciously remember. I closed my eyes, and hesitantly raised each hand to the keyboard, and suddenly both of my forefingers hit two "C's" simultaneously and immediately took me away into blooming fields of classic perfection.

Clearly, I used to be so afraid I wouldn't remember what I needed to know, or have the courage to do what I needed to do. However, little did I know that scary night began the *making of me*. In those uncertain moments, I began to grow guts in the pit of my belly that would serve me well for the rest of my life. Courage and grit, born that night, became my two true friends. They have continued to buoy me through many uncertainties and challenges, foibles and successes.

No matter how scary the vacant piano bench is, or how complex the "epilogue" is that I need to play, I am confident now that I have what I need to place my hands on the keys of my life and play confidently with passion and verve. You see, I have learned to wipe the sweat of my palms on my pretty britches, calm my knocking knees, kick off the white high heel shoes, and walk masterfully—barefoot and with tits up, across the stage of my life. Besides, now having faith in myself, I get that I will know whatever I need to do!

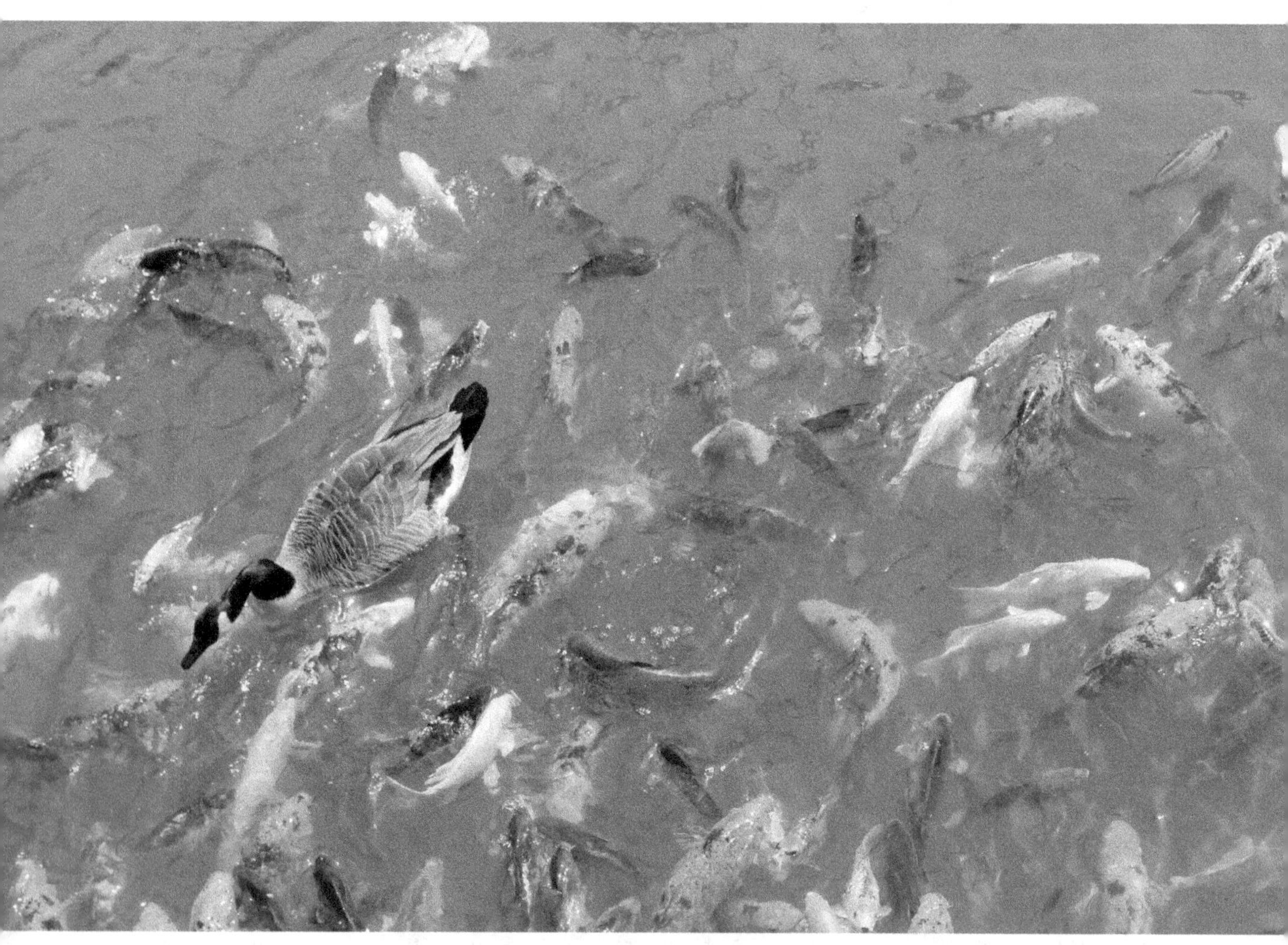

Duck Among Fish

Ellie Godwin

(Definition of) Summer

Todd Robinson

Every morning the same fuckup,
but whose abacus ticks the hits,
as if some astral martinet tsks
my eight-am bong habit, equates
it to the clowns and midgets
my buddy 'bates to on sin.com.
Thirty years ago I found myself
in the parental closet, mom's
dresses phantoming above me,
dad's silk shirts pre-cologned
for who-knows-what. You think
that's the story, just wait:
underneath their second skins,
boxes and boxes of vintage
Playboys, soft-focus Venuses
bending to my raking gaze.
I have no idea what all those
jeweled gams have to do
with my morning brain scramble.
What sort of things scald your
past? Did you lean over your
lawn chair in a drunken swoon
and tell your best friend you'd
do him, if the stars were right?

When he joked about bringing
his essential oils to the male
bonding party, did he mean it?
No one has ever liked my what-ifs.
I line up the strings of possible
selves and everybody gets nervous,
but truly we could play all sorts
of banjos, make our fingers bleed
unreadable glyphs on the tits
of femmes and doms alike. We're
that free, in theory. Load another
bowl and you'll forget the forking
paths, watch the long grass loll
while your little boy self plays
Red Rover in the basement
of a house you still drive by
every week, the ghost of your
teenage self headbanging
himself vodka-sick in the same
space, all these nesting dolls
spilling from the mouth of time.
But I'm having some difficulty.
Parsing the meatus of leisure time
in a meaningful way means
staying above ground while humidity
batters the windows, the phone
quiet as a prairie graveyard.
You can go walking through
the stones, even read the names,
but no one's whispering in your ear.
You think that cricket mantra
is the voice of God? Think again.

After an hour with the girls,
sweating it out nigh all that beauty,
I closed up the box and reeled
back to my room, bone-hard
and haunted. How was I to resume
my boyhood after such a shock?
It is impossible to be the person
we want to be. To keep ourselves
out of the basement, the closet,
the arms of summer. Or to know
why we were led to believe
in perfectibility. Or to say no
to the fire burning our lips
we have wanted so long to taste.

Event of the Century

Bridgit Kuenning-Pollpeter

Winter wind whips my long hair about me as I tap my long white cane against the brick wall of Fuddrucker's, searching for the door. My friends do the same with their canes. Grease filters through the chilly air—the unmistakable odor of a burger joint. We're cold and hungry, and finding the door, we scurry inside.

Seven friends out on a Saturday having a good time, and we all happen to be blind.

We pile into the entrance, tapping our white canes to investigate the restaurant. Ross, my husband, and I find a wall and follow it tapping back-and-forth with our canes.

"Hey guys," I call out, "I believe this is the counter."

The click of cane tips echoes from multiple directions as Shane, Amy, Audra, Jamie and Carol find their way to the counter. Since the menu is not available in Braille, we ask the cashier to please read the choices out loud.

We place our respective orders, some of us pulling out credit cards, others rifling through cash identifying bills based on how the denominations are folded.

I grab my cup and listen for the soda fountain. Ice chinks into a cup and I follow the sound. An island separates the soda fountain from where I stand; I pause, determining which direction to move. Before I can take another step though, a stranger approaches me.

"Can I help you?" she asks.

"No thanks." Stepping around the stranger, arcing my cane, I can tell she's hesitating. I ignore her and continue moving around the island, tapping it with my cane.

The stranger pinches a fold of my coat and yanks me around the island. "It's this way."

"Thanks, but that's the direction I was moving in, ma'am." I'm thrown off balance from being tugged about, but I stand upright, and adjust my jacket. My cheeks are flushed, and my chest tightens as I take deep, slow breaths.

She pauses as six other blind people move past in a flying-V, seeking an open table.

"Where is your companion?" she asks. Her voice is filled with concern and hesitation.

I hold my breath, purse my lips, and say, "Well, seeing as we're all adults, we don't have a companion." I follow the cane taps, leaving the stranger alone to ponder the miracle happening before her eyes.

"The freak show's out. Everyone should grab their camera," Audra says as I approach the table. We all quietly chuckle.

We don't mean to be rude, but we're all use to this reaction when in public. The amazing blind people who have left the security of their homes. How do we manage?

Encountering ridiculous ideas and outdated attitudes towards blindness in nearly every setting keeps my cynicism fresh.

As I left campus one day, a man approached me from behind declaring, "You are amazing."

"What do you mean?"

"You get around so well. It's truly amazing you can walk."

"Thanks, but I'm blind, not paralyzed."

"I just mean it's amazing you don't run into stuff."

"If I didn't use this cane, I would run into everything." I sighed and proceeded down the stairs leading to a parking lot.

The man followed me and stopped just feet away from where I stood waiting for my ride; he was captivated by finding a real, live blind person, as though I were a rare bird.

Snow sifted from the sky kissing my head and face. I turned and said, "It's snowing again."

"See, you're amazing. How do you know it's snowing? It must be your sixth sense."

"Noooo, I feel it. Can't you?"

Eight years ago, I didn't think the hardest part of being blind would be dealing with society's perceptions and attitudes. I accept it just as I accept the color of my hair or my inability to solve a math equation quickly. Others, though, think it is all I am.

It's difficult to be around people, not because I have problems with my blindness, but because others do. I'm no longer just a person; I'm now a blind person. Many can't get past the white cane, choosing to see what they want to see. Perhaps they are the ones who are blind. I'm human, a person with thoughts, likes and dislikes, emotions, passions; I just happen to be blind.

I'd rather spend time with children. They have an innate ability to trust and not doubt because of a perceived reality. My favorite pastime is spending time with my nephew and nieces. I must have the baby bug or something—the biological clock. Tick, tick, tick.

Caiden is seven and a bit too smart for his own good. Chloe is six, extremely independent and loves with her whole heart. Kensley is almost three, and she has the sweetest temperament; but every now and then, she gets a wild, mischievous glimmer in her eyes. Penny is two, full of energy, and makes me more like a mom than an aunt.

I've watched them evolve from tiny beings, into real people, and it is through them I see where the future can be. I'm often met with dubious stares and hesitant comments while watching the kids.

"How can you watch children?"

"Isn't it difficult?"

"How can blind people do that?"

Once, during a phone conversation with a family member, I mentioned how people often seem uncomfortable with Ross and me babysitting the kids. The response was, "Well, can you blame them?"

Yes, as a matter of fact, I can. People can be so insulting, whether they realize it or not. Why am I expected to accept ignorant attitudes because, "People just don't know better," but no one is expected to accept me as a capable adult? Is it really asking too much? It's a simple equation.

When I take the kids to the park or the mall or on a walk, people tend to assume the kids are guiding me around. Yes, a seven-year-old, six-year-old, three-year-old and a two-year-old guide me. We would all be dead.

The kids never question my abilities though. Blindness is normal to them. My actions speak volumes to them. We think children have mental limitations, but they understand what adults cannot. My babies accept me and don't doubt their safety with me.

Caiden loves video games. If allowed, he'd play them all day. Once, my mom, in an attempt to get him to stop playing and go outside, stated, "If you play too many video games you will go blind."

His response, delivered in a simple dry tone, was, "Grandma, it's not a big deal to be blind. Look at Aunt Bridgy."

Through these words, the impact of my actions is evident. These children take what I do and say at face-value instead of acting upon societal perceptions and questioning me. They are the beginning of a generation that can break the stereotypes about blindness.

Recently Chloe has taken to walking around with her eyes closed because she "wants to be like Aunt Bridgy."

She often grabs a white cane to walk with when visiting. She's also fascinated with Braille, wanting to learn this tactile form of print. Everywhere she goes, she points out signs that have Braille on them. She has no fear. To Chloe, blindness is just another way to "be."

Kensley and Penny are still grasping the fact that I don't respond to visual cues, like nodding their heads. Both have quickly adjusted to finding other means in which to express their wants.

They toddle to me placing their arms around my legs, wanting to be held. When they want to show me a toy, they place it in my hands.

Children don't question my ability to care for them. To them, I'm comfort, I'm love, I'm security, and of course, I'm the lady who can dole out food.

Sometimes, I pin a small bell to the back of their clothing to identify where they are, but usually their gibber-jabber pinpoints their location. As Penny and Kensley's vocabulary grows, they will understand they must use their words, and not gestures, to communicate with me. These two will grow up never thinking I'm odd, or doubt I can care for them.

Adults, on the other hand, don't always see beyond my blindness. True, not everyone buys into the antiquated stereotypes, and not everyone believes me inferior, but, in my experience, most people still cling to old notions.

Shortly after our wedding, Ross and I ran errands one weekend. Waiting for a bus, holding hands, we discussed our plans for the day.

Snow crunched beneath my rubber galoshes as I jumped up and down to keep warm. Ross laughed pulling me into a bear hug. Smiling, I rubbed my frozen, pug nose against his angular one.

Bus brakes screeched a block away. I whooped, relieved we would be on a warm bus soon. As the bus jolted to a stop in front of us, a whoosh of air blew my scarf up around my face.

We swiped our bus passes, then tapped our canes across the seats searching for empty spots; we reveled in the hot air blasting from the vents.

As the bus lurched, Ross reached his arm around my shoulders, made bulky from my winter jacket. We carried on our discussion, grazing our tingling hands together.

Shouting over the din of the bus, a woman cut into our conversation. "You're a beautiful couple."

I smiled in her direction, and thanked her, then turned back to Ross.

“Which assisted living do you live in?” the woman asked.

Cocking my head at a slight angle, I felt my lips grow thin and my brow furl. “Excuse me? Us?”

“Yes. I wondered which assisted living facility you live in.”

“What makes you assume we live in an assisted living facility?” I asked.

Her voice faltered. “You’re blind—don’t you, um, I mean… Does someone just live with you?”

I gripped Ross’s arm, my face flushed. Narrowing my eyes, I skimmed through possible answers.

I squeezed myself into him, his leg pumping in a restless up and down motion, and absent-mindedly fiddling with the wedding ring on my finger, Ross spoke. “We live on our own. No one checks up on us, no one lives with us.”

“Oh. That’s amazing.” The woman trailed off, remaining silent the rest of the trip.

Diplomacy is the usual route I take, but there are times when I can no longer deal with the attitudes forced on me. I try to educate—I try to be positive, but watch out if you catch me on a bad day.

One day, I stood at the curb waiting to cross the street. Focused on the sound of traffic in front of me on Center Street, and adjacent traffic to my right on Paddock road, I prepared to cross.

I know how long I have to zip across when the light changes. The red light holds me captive—takes forever to change. Once it switches, there’s only fifteen-seconds allotted to cross four lanes of traffic and navigate a median.

Come on. I tapped my long white cane on the pavement out of boredom.

Suddenly, a crazed pedestrian grabbed my elbow from behind, forcing me into oncoming traffic. I had no choice but to keep truckin’ to the other side, terrified to stop amid the zooming cars.

After reaching the other side, I slapped the strangers hand away and shouted, “What the hell are you doing?”

“Are you good?” Crazy asked, ignoring my question.

“Are you insane? You can see, right? Clearly, we did not have the right of way. Shit! You could have killed us both. I wasn’t looking to die today.”

Crazy, who I swore was looking to meet her fate back out on Center Street, grabbed for my arm again.

I grabbed her wrist and asked, "Do I know you? No, so what gives you the idea I want a complete stranger touching me?"

"Can you make it home from here?"

I stared in her direction. Can she hear? "Uh, I think I'm good. How the hell do you think I was getting around before you, like a maniac, dragged me across the street?"

"Have a good day. Sure, you can get home okay?"

"I shouted, OH MY GOD!" I turned, stomping my feet hard against the concrete toward my apartment complex, gently tapping my cane in front of me.

I was safely and cautiously waiting to cross a busy city street. She assumed I was incapable for some reason. She placed me, and herself, into a dangerous situation. Instead of thinking, "Hmm, this person is blind, but she is out and about on her own, she must be okay. She appears to know what she is doing." But no, she only "sees" the blind girl standing alone and can't get past that thought.

Yes, I had to learn how to get around safely way back when, but I get around 24 hours every freaking day, 365 days, 31.5 million seconds a year. What does she think I do the rest of those seconds without her? Is this my one moment outside where I bravely escaped into the big bad dangerous world and I was so damn lucky she was there to save me in that five second exchange? Thank God, she was there! Only another, well, 31,499,995 more seconds to go this year.

My friends all have similar stories. We're seven people enjoying each other's company, but because we're all blind, it's considered the event of the century to venture out into the world.

We range in age from twenty-five to thirty-five. Some of us have children, all of us work. Four of us are social workers, one an accountant, one a writer and one a computer technician. A couple of us girls wear make-up and stay current with fashion trends. The guys are avid sports nuts, especially when it comes to collegiate football. Despite being adults who do adult things, it is considered an awesome accomplishment that we're socializing without a sighted companion.

It is even more incredible that our conversation sounds like any other conversation. The girls chatter about what to do at the mall, and the guys shout out comments about the football game blaring on the television. Our server is confused.

"You're all blind, right?" she asks.

Seven voices chorus, "YES!"

Fly, Once

Maritza N. Estrada

Runners take laps around the blue-green dyed
        lake, construction crew in orange shirts
who've been at work since dawn,
                & mother ducks nestled to their kin.

Who knows how many hours have passed
        when my eyes meet a premature robin
                                        on cement stair-
                                                    steps,
                        breathing in   breaths—
ribcage extending like an ajo lily,   lungs rising &
                                                    falling.
Pink-
waxen skin is a membrane. Black
                                        bulging eyes
                                        bigger than a marble-
                                                    head.
When a robin is born, both eyes see magnetic fields—
patterns of light & shade.

Must it have been today? Death & death.
                                        A corpse is located deep,
deep, deep,
        in the indigo
   bottom.

Myself by the robin's side, whispering,
          Keep breathing.

The rescue crew arrives
& I believe they are here for you. "Leave the scene,
leave the scene," they say, "Shoo."
                                        & I remain waiting for
your rescue, frantic & sitting, watching
                                        the stillness
of a human body pulled from the blue-green dyed lake—
                        sun rays refract away from ripples,
water & air, water &
                        air, water
                        & air.
Yellow tape closes the area.   *Breathe.*

When the evening's passed under white moonlight,
          shade & light, an aurora of vision,
say where you flew.

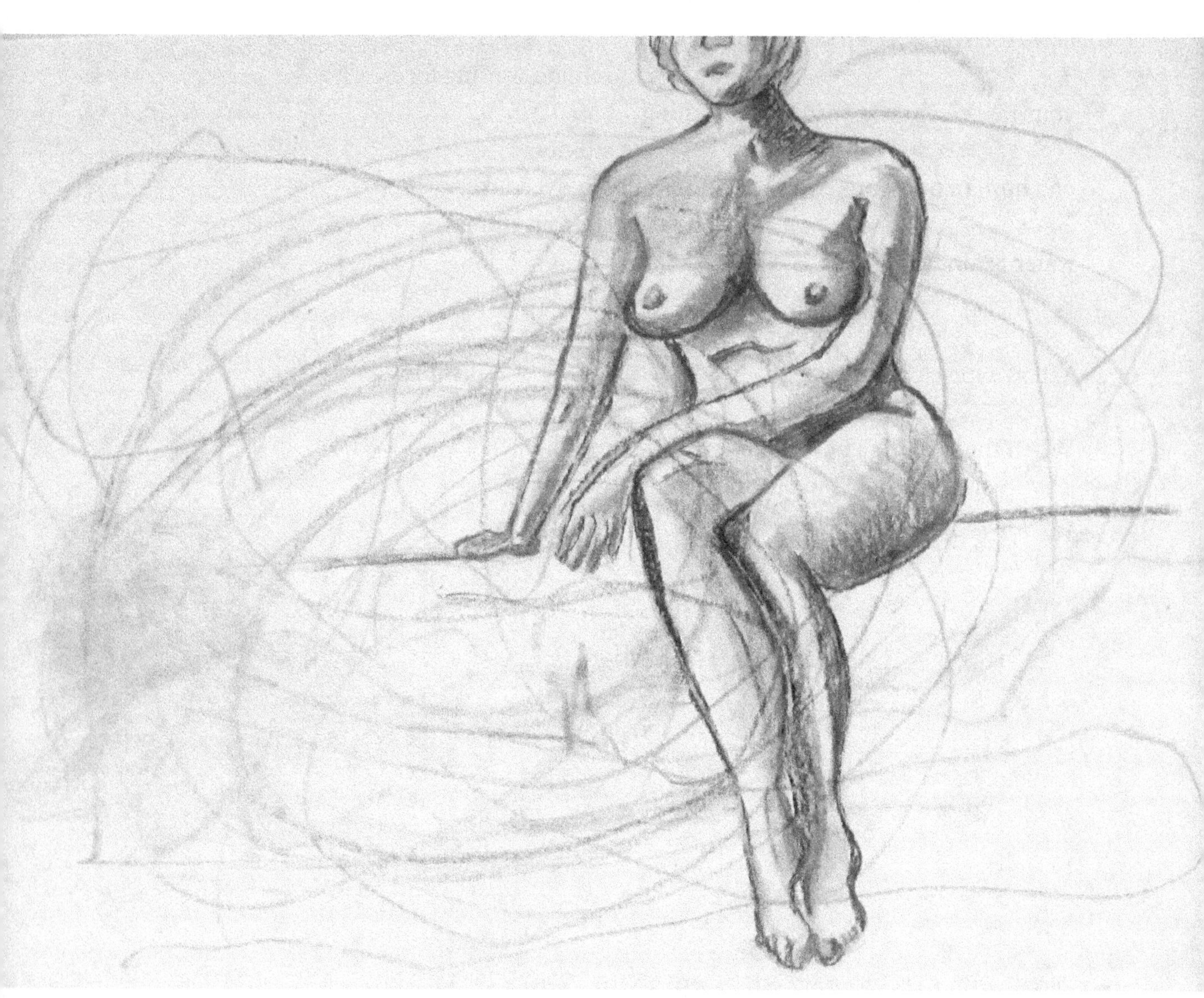

Kristin Resting

Sally Deskins

A Difficult Poem

Deirdre Evans

This is a difficult poem.
It won't take advice, it talks out of turn.
It eats that last piece of cake you were saving for yourself,
and blames it on the dog.
If you turn your back on it, even for an instant,
this poem will stop,
grab any old cliché
and smell it like a rose.

This poem has limitations.
It cannot bring back the dead.
It squints when reading the fine print
and never knows what day it is.
It has a hard time getting dressed
from its closet-full of adjectives
found in a thrift-store thesaurus.
This poem is a fussy eater
and has been known to spit out green peppers.

This poem has ambitions.
It wants to be listed in the credits
as Best Boy or Make-Up Artist.
It wants to be a glitter rock star
with back-up singers and a cute drummer.
This poem would like a footnote,
in italics, to praise its rise to fame.

This poem has made an effort
and hopes you notice it looks pretty.
This poem is willing to go home with you.

Exorcism

Michael Skau

Driving across Nebraska, mind shuffled
by endlessly riffling rows of young corn,
window arm raw red from the all-day sun,
windshield spattered in streaks yellow and white
by butterfly wings and bug guts. Abrupt
evening slams down, twilight figures ghostly
fading from hard edge to soft and then back
again, like memories of love, wandering
lady, dancing to tunes as old as the night,
while every new guy caught her eye like soap,
a flower to every passing bee–God, no!
The image must be savage, more stinking:
a sewer that sucks from any flushing pipe.
The twilight fades to calm, to easeful dark.

Guitar

Charlene Pierce

Why did you leave me here all alone?

You hold me so carefully. At first touch you glide your hand down my body, as if to make sure I'm okay. I can tell you missed me too. You take a moment to feel me, connect with me, become in tune with me. Then you place your hands on me with all the passion and love you have stored in your heart, and I come alive in your hands.

We become one with my body cradled in yours. You know how to play me just right. When to go slow and caress my neck, when to pick up the tempo and dance with me, making us sing out loud, creating a sound and rhythm that is unique and all ours.

The love we have for each other radiates out and brings people to us. They can't help but be drawn in by us. They want to laugh with us, cry with us, share in our music, feeling all we have to give. Why are we not giving now?

Where did you go?

Don't you know that you need me as much as I need you?

When you are gone, I am left here lifeless and still. Because you wander and continue to laugh and play, you convince yourself that you are okay. But you are not fully alive until you are with me. With me, you are open and free.

Come back to me Jon.

Come back and make me sing.

Anxiety

Sheila Hansen

It's like living in the space
between the lightning and thunder. The light,
there just long enough to show you the deluge
and strip you of any acclimation to the dark, is gone.

You're left blinking away the afterimage and counting.
Desperately counting distance in the dark.
Skin crawling with escaping electricity
and anticipation.

Bracing for the bone-shaking boom you know is coming.
Hoping for the rolling growl
of retreat you've only dreamt about.
You've long forgotten the calm before your storm,
and you know now
those blue-sky sunshine memories are just the lies
you told yourself to drown out wind-whipped howling.

You exist only in moments amidst the chaos,
the occasional shaking breath of stillness waiting to be
broken.
You're soaked in dread;
and it weighs heavier than the water-logged chill
and suffocating cling of your clothes ever could.

Every shrinking moment between the numbers itches
with the fearful certainty that you will count no higher.
This count will stop sooner than the last.
They always do.
This achingly terrible limbo shrinks with every flash, and
everything within you both rejoices in
and recoils from that knowledge.

There will come a moment when
there is no time for counting,
when the crowding static
dissipated by the previous crash of sound will flood back
so quickly
it will prick its way underneath your skin
to meet the thunder waiting in your veins.

In that moment,
you'll be left at zero with nothing left to ground you.

The fracturing flash of that impact will
burn away the numbers and the hair-raising buzz
of energy trapped in inactive trepidation
leaving nothing
but a blinding heat to illuminate the encircling downpour.

That's the finale to an act not yet written.
In this fleeting intermission,
a brief moment pulled like taffy
in the aching stretch between
a gladiatorial flash of challenge and the battering echo
of collision,

there is nothing but darkness
and the distant sound of sirens as they begin to count.

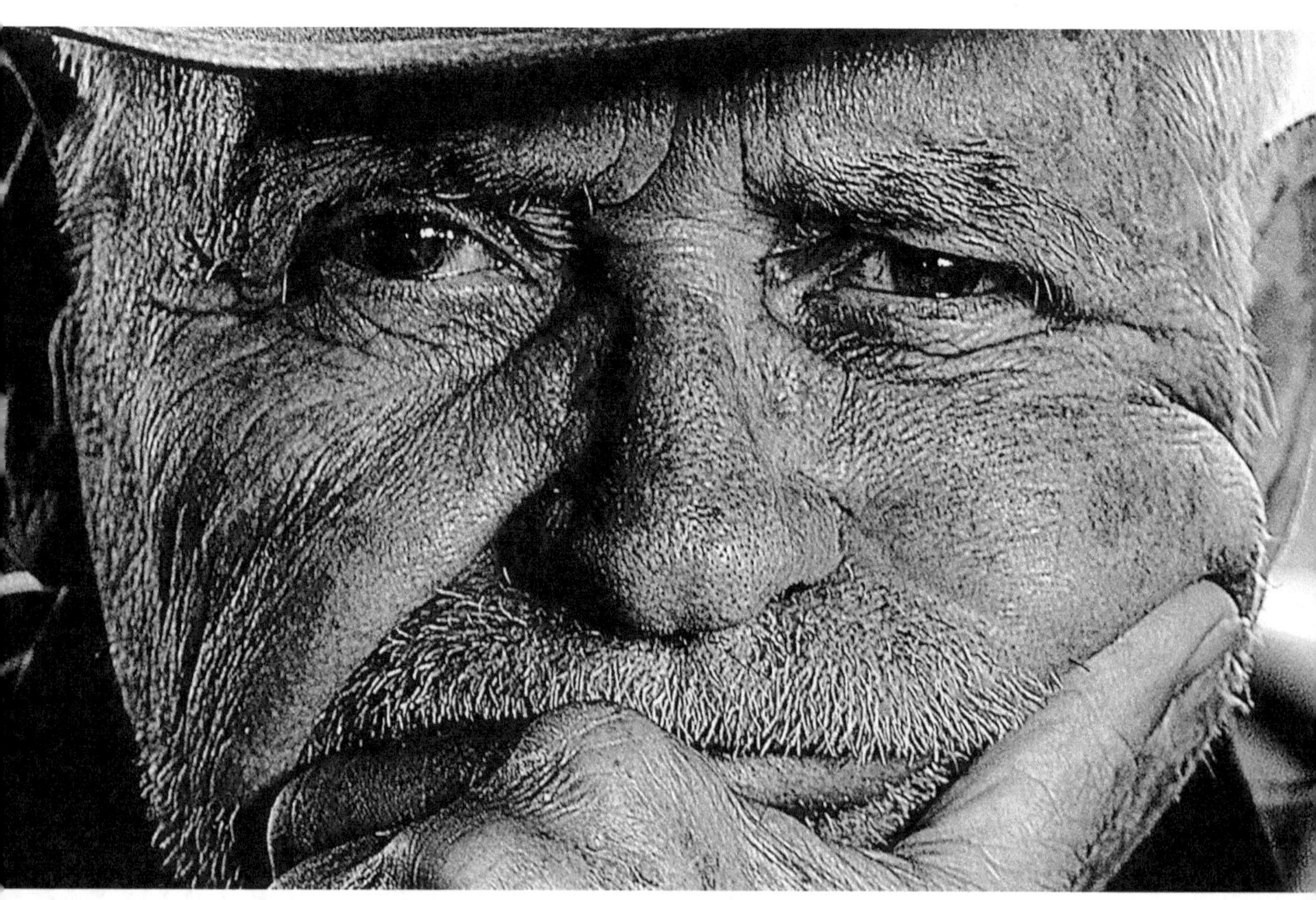

Rough Going

Bob Spittler

Hangover

Connie Spittler

The cowboy tried to shake off his morning headache as he gazed over the campfire.
He wished on a pale piece of moon that hung on a hunk of Nebraska sky.
"Where does the moon go?" He'd asked his mama all those years ago.
And she told him, "It's circling us, earth and moon connected, busy circling the sun.
An endless circling of the universe. Circles within circles within circles."
The thought made him stand up slowly to escape the dizziness inside.
He warmed up yesterday's coffee, marking the beginning of his hangover chase.
After running his hand over the worn ax handle, he tested the blade.
In no time, he found his groove, splitting logs,
The rhythm of arm and shoulder swinging in time.
The curve of the ax bit into the wood.
The smell of pine needles swept out the effect of high octane booze
from last night's fall from grace.
Now oxygen from deep breathing passed through his chest, air healing body parts.
The pale bit of moon faded, taking with it this morning's dull suffering.
He was saved.
Once more, he'd escaped from a night on the town, with the memory of
Wet circles within circles of empty beer glasses that signaled too much brew.
The endless circling of his saloon universe.
And he felt assured his salvation would last and last and last,
At least until the next time.

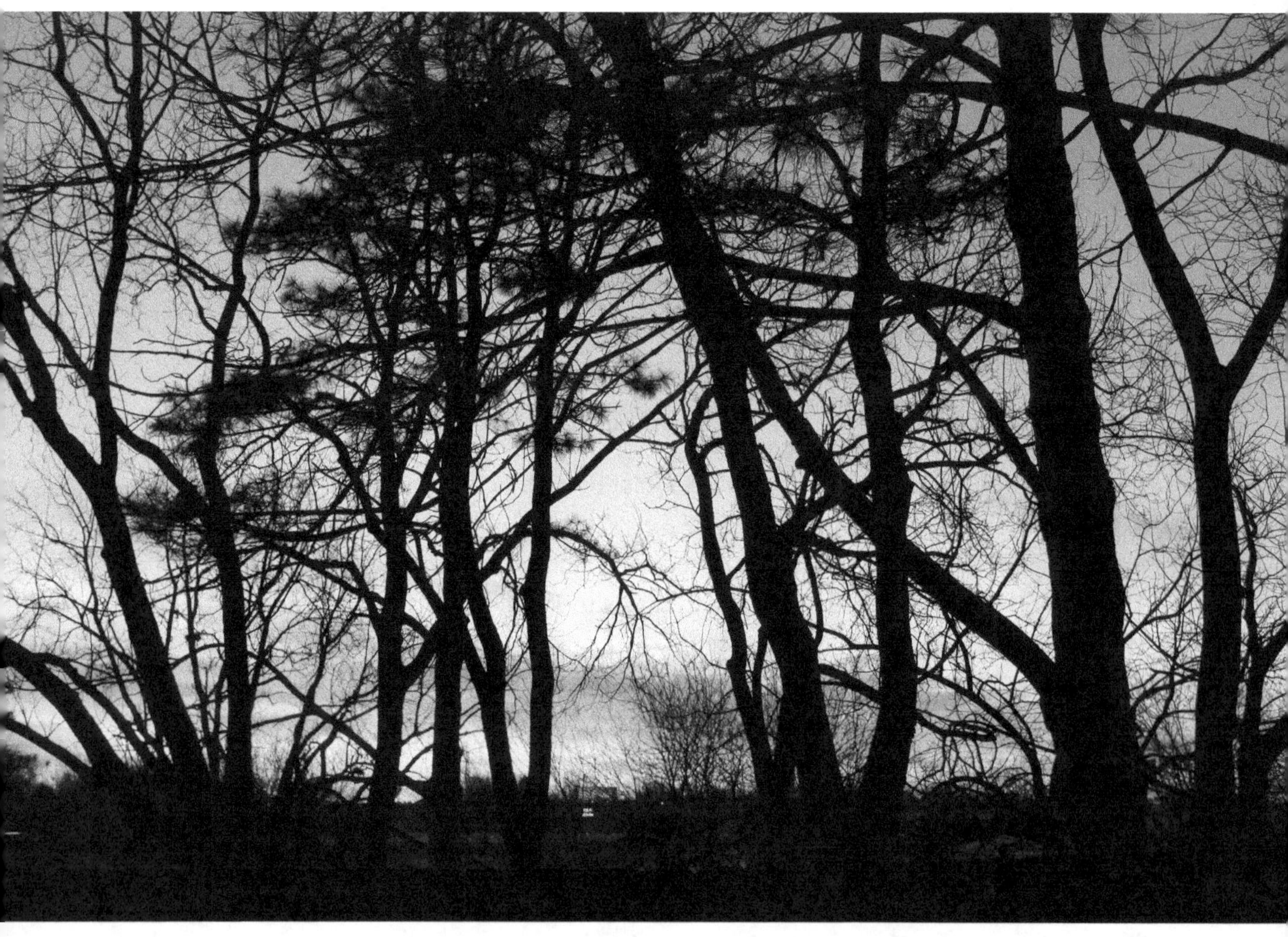

Sunrise in Omaha

Ellie Godwin

Old Hens

Marilyn Dorf

Always, they were called old.
But whether they were old or not,
those hens strode out of their coop
refreshed every morning, ready for
a new day. Exclaiming. Proclaiming.
Declaring their space on the planet,
as they roamed the farmyard, chasing
grasshoppers, butterflies, mosquitoes,
snatching up berries and stray bits
of corn. On steamy, hot afternoons,
they sifted themselves into the dust
they had scratched beneath the old elm,
lowering themselves into the sweet cool
of the earth, chittering, chirping,
one to another, as ladies at tea,
soaking up each day to its limit,
never knowing which one might
be served up for dinner on Sunday—
and tomorrow already Saturday…
then at dusk they headed back to their
coop, wings fluffed like shawls, as if
sneaking bright berries of sunshine
into the dimness of dark.

Gone

Charlene Pierce

Wiped the dust off my iPod and turned it on full blast. I can still hear enough of the bass to remember Annie Lennox's haunting voice.

"*. . . A thousand beautiful things . . .*"

How much longer... a month... a year, until I can't hear the bass either? Will the vibrations of it be enough to remind me of all the notes in between? I place my hand over the speaker in my ear and try to implant the notes with the beats in my mind. You, Steven, would think it silly of me to keep listening to Annie Lennox when I can no longer hear her resonating voice.

Your music, I would love to see again. I wanted to see you perform so badly. Your music is so important to you and I wanted you to share it with me. You were hesitant to take me. Joking that taking a date to your show is bad for groupies. You made me laugh. You made me smile. So much laughter we shared. Yet I knew you were worried about me not having fun, thinking that someone who can't fully hear the music can't fully enjoy it.

"*. . . Light me up like the sun . . .*"

I can still see you singing, standing tall, strong, soft spotlight shining across your shoulders. Arms open wide, as if you are letting the music in. The passion in you as you thump the meaning out on your chest with your fist. Reading your lips and seeing more than the words. That was the moment I knew I had fallen for you. Women all around me were swooning over you. They didn't have the privilege to see what I saw; your strong heart that's been broken and mended and filled with passion. A heart that is open and ready to love and be loved. When you love, you will hide nothing. You will love completely; and it won't be with me.

"*. . . It's mine to remember now . . .*"

You asked me, "If I can't share my music with you, how can I share me with you?" Told me our intimacy is lost because you can't say the things to me that can only be said under the covers in the darkness of the bedroom.

Whisper to me. Don't stop. The feeling of your voice, your breath, your lips on my ear leave me wanting and wet. Kiss me with your eyes open. Show me the words. Do you want me? Pull me closer to you. Do you think I am sexy? Show me. Glide your hand across me, down the hollow of my back, up the curve of my hip, across my stomach, the arch of my breast, my nipples hard for you at your touch, envelop my throat, brush my cheek and through my hair with the tug of passion. Can you feel me? Do I need words?

". . . Never close my eyes. . .
Never
Close
My
Eyes"

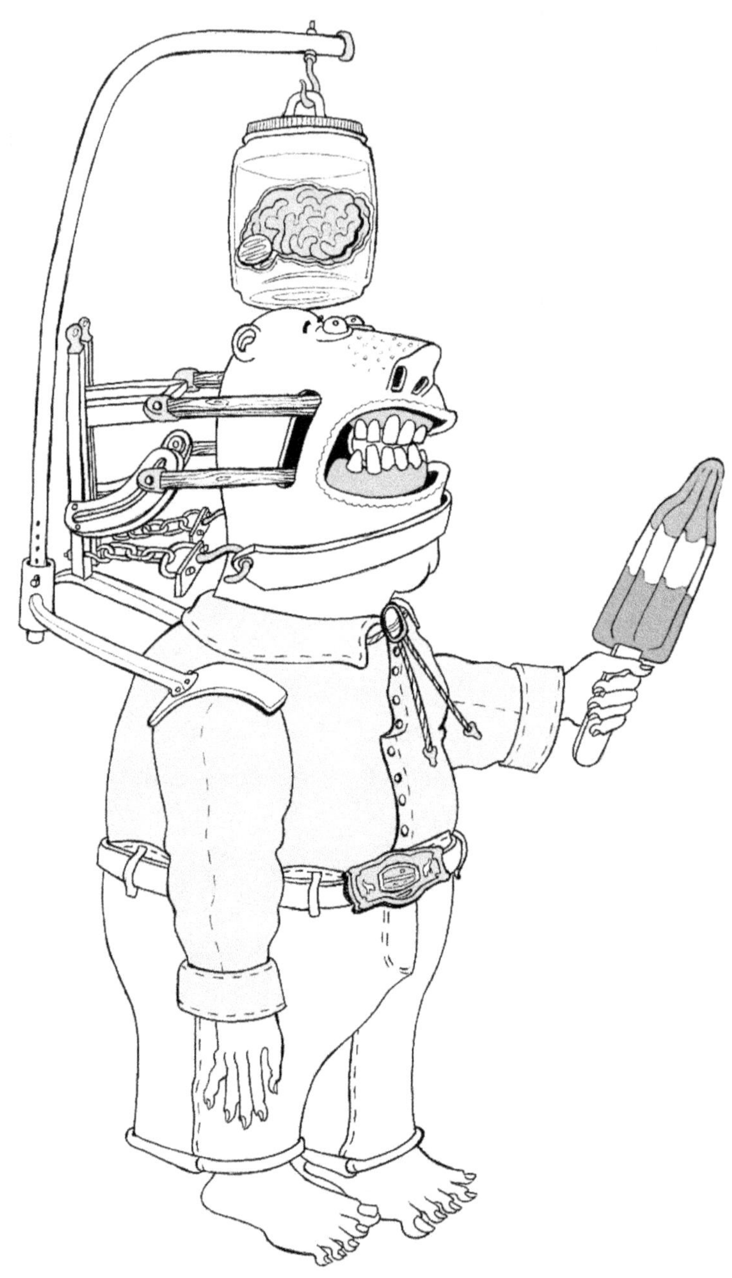

bomb pop

Joe Pankowski

Her Art

Clif Mason
for Cat Dixon

The sky was the black of necrotic flesh.
Amid broken concrete slabs and shattered
glass, rabbits still bred. Strolling the streets
between vertigo and vagrancy, she stopped
in an alley to watch night open like a vast
chrysalis and bring mutant insects
into the world. Chemicals diffused into air
and water made bodies blacken like mold-
covered walls. As the moon's dead cylinder
floated off, blue light poured down
the mountain and rolled off horses' backs
like steam. It filled the spaces between trees
and immured campers like volcanic ash.

She wanted the horse with teeth like stars,
with a mane and tail like the fall of snow.
Its back was broad as a blue whale's,
its feet fleet as a cheetah's. Its hooves echoed
like talking drums. She called but it heard
sorrow clinging like mistletoe to her voice
and wouldn't come. She called again, this time
with a tone clear as a river of subterranean
water. The horse neighed and cantered
across night's pastures to her side.
She knew, whatever her grief, she must sing,
though her song scalded the eyes, sing,
though it boiled the heart in its bloody cauldron.

Upon Viewing Renaissance Art at the Joslyn

F. Patrick Stehno

The sure smell of religion;
Renaissance art.
She nearly genuflected
when she entered the gallery,
felt the sting of burnt cedar
upon her tongue,
the pain of guilt and catechism.
The taste of holy oils and inquisition.

Too many Catholic ceremonies
and papal institutions
deflecting the brush
from a true-to-life Virgin.
Always pale, washed out, sexless;
as the Church appeared to be
but never was.

Satin Dreams

Michael Skau

I bought a set of satin sheets, a fitted
heaven, or so I thought, for our love, and dreamed
a bodied angel tucked into a cloud
of royal blue, gold hair and love-firm flesh
cushioned on satin lush, textures to tempt
God Himself, soft as a whisper fireplace nights,
plush and cool, a lake stocked with pleasure, deep
as lust and just as pure, rippling with sex.

But damn if when we climbed inside those sheets
that bed-world didn't warp and plunge awry:
the pillows leapt the edge like suicides
as blankets avalanched. Then we lay, heads
bolstered on arms and shoulders, bodies huddled
against the night into each other's passion.

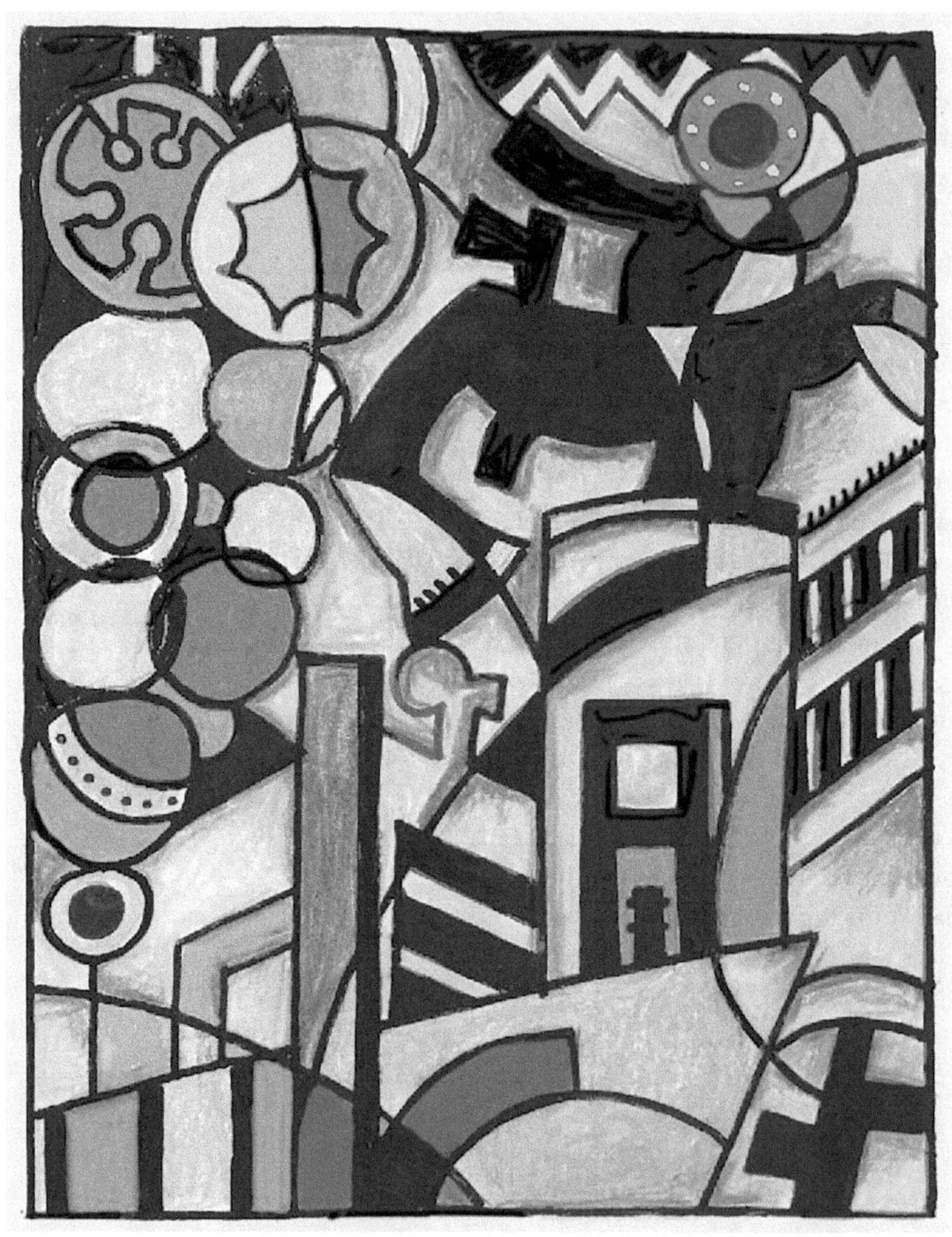

Homage to Sarah Joslyn

Robert Klein Engler

I Left Him There

Marjorie Saiser

That day was a sunny day,
the kind he must have liked,
a meadowlark out of sight in tall grass,
the song sprinkling over prairie country.
Seedheads of brome stirring,
resting a little, stirring again.
What is not seen is wind,
his kindness, or his hand
holding a wrench or hammer,
lifting a concrete block,
sanding seams of plasterboard.
Some things you never see again.
Today the ground is so hard
I have to empty my water bottle
over the spot where I want to
stake the wreath down, soften
the earth, push in the wire that will
hold the yellow plastic flowers
in the wind, the blue ribbon flapping.
Brome grass just north of his plot
still moves as if
a hand ruffled it, stirred it,
loved the feel of it
for a moment and then
there was nothing but to go on.

Imagine Blue

Charlene Pierce

Think blue. Blue, soft and light—like a feather… drifting, drifting down in a warm summer breeze, or like angel wings floating up and up into the soft blue sky. Soft blue air floats by me, through my hair, between my arms, over my stomach, moving between my legs, wrapping around my ankles. It's graceful, like the soft back of a hand gently, slowly moving down the side of my breast… soft, like the tip of an angel's wings.

Not like Nick's calloused hands scratching me. Nick, coarse and hard, set in stone.

"You get off work at 3, you should be home by 3:37," he says.

Can't stop at the store, must go home first. What if he needs something? He is mad that I'm not home. I am late, five minutes, five hours; it doesn't matter. The punishment is the same. But I was already in trouble anyway. It doesn't get any worse and I am tired. I want to sit here for a while and lay my legs on the moist sand.

Imagine white soft sand, like clouds… big, fluffy, airy clouds. The tiny white granules of sand glisten with sun and moisture. Like dew on a bright clear morning it wakes me, makes me feel alive. It is cool and moist, like soft vanilla ice cream. It's soft and giving, like quicksand with support somewhere underneath not letting me drown. It caresses my body like a white velvet beanbag, accepting me… holding me.

Unlike Nick, who grabs rough and holds hard. Reaching quick like lightning, out of nowhere it seems. Sometimes he strikes from behind me, grabbing me as I walk by. His hands clutch around my arm, tight like a trap. He jerks me toward him. I lose my balance. He squishes my body so that I breathe like a patient with emphysema, quick and shallow breaths. My face presses up against his shoulder, hard bone driving into my cheek…

Think blue. Blue water… ocean water, ocean water with foam that is white and fluffy like the top of a lemon meringue pie, as it floats around the water it whispers across my skin. I close my eyes and take in a deep cool breath of ocean air, moist, salty air. Not salty sweat that stings the scratches on my arms and thighs. The scratches

Nick gave me the last time I was in trouble. I thought when we married things would be different. But I'm still in trouble most of the time.

The first time Nick was mad at me, he shoved me across the room. I slipped and went sliding across the carpet. My face slammed into the bottom of the couch. It didn't break my nose, but I had two black eyes anyway. He didn't mean to shove me so hard, and it's not his fault that I fell. That was when we were first married. I wanted to take a night job at the hospital.

"At night, a wife should be home with the husband," he said.

I don't go anywhere though, just work and then home. But today I came here. I was already in trouble.

Here, I want it blue, serene, calm, and clean—like a fresh dip in a pool… floating, floating, down while the water relaxes me, lightly sustains me. My arms and legs stretch out feeling the massaging weight of the water, moving the water, moving through it by waving my arms and legs, changing the pressure as I move. My hair waves and mixes with the cool water while its soft force brushes across my face, tickling my eyelashes and caressing my cheeks. Soft splashes across my skin, not stinging slaps like I'll get when I get home. They moved me to the night shift. Nick will be mad. I want to stay here and dip my feet in the water.

Think blue, soft blue, like my silk hair ribbon gliding across the nape of my neck before Nick snatched it out of my hand. Why was I in trouble that time? What did I do? That's why I'm always in trouble; I can't remember all the things I have to stop doing wrong. Makeup is for sluts. Or, does makeup make me look like a slut? I can't remember which. I want to stay here where it is… too pretty. I think that was one of the nights that I was too pretty.

I wish that water stayed blue, all the way through. But it turns green when it gets deep, an icky mossy green. It would be so pretty if ocean water turned deep blue instead of green, deep blue like a blue jay or a blueberry. Then I could wade out into the water and it would be like wading out into royal blue velvet, or like wading into a sapphire geode, crystalline and pure.

But it isn't like that, especially here at Salt Lake. Salt Lake is grey and dingy, dirty grey sand, dead grey water. Here it is all dead, or rather, nothing ever lived. I can't drown here. All that salt keeps me up, makes me float. I just bob in the water unable to go down, down to the bottom of the lake. But there is nothing at the bottom anyway. Nothing can live in all that salt.

Up North

Pat Hazell

Bursting through sugar maples,
Palm of Michigan's hand. Poplars applaud.
Handcrafted birdhouses guard oatmeal skies.

Orphaned Christmas saplings
Sketch shadows down the drive; gravel
  GuRfliNKs
      off wheel wells…
Thigh-high hayfields host
A symphony of cicadas.
An abandoned pontoon beckons at pond's edge.

Frog-dappled creek
    staggers
              drunkenly
        toward
Root cellar bloated with pickled treats.
Sweet smells of oily wood saturate the workshop.
The resident lumberjack chops mechanically
through gust and gale.
Cribbage and cabbage await.

Fresh cream floats in clear narrow necks;
Cinnamon rolls swing dance deftly in the breeze.
Amber and cobalt sun-catchers line
shelter's belly; juggling
sun rays floor to ceiling.

Silent is dinner bell's song,
Absent are quilted embraces.
Vacancy signs adorn hearth and home.

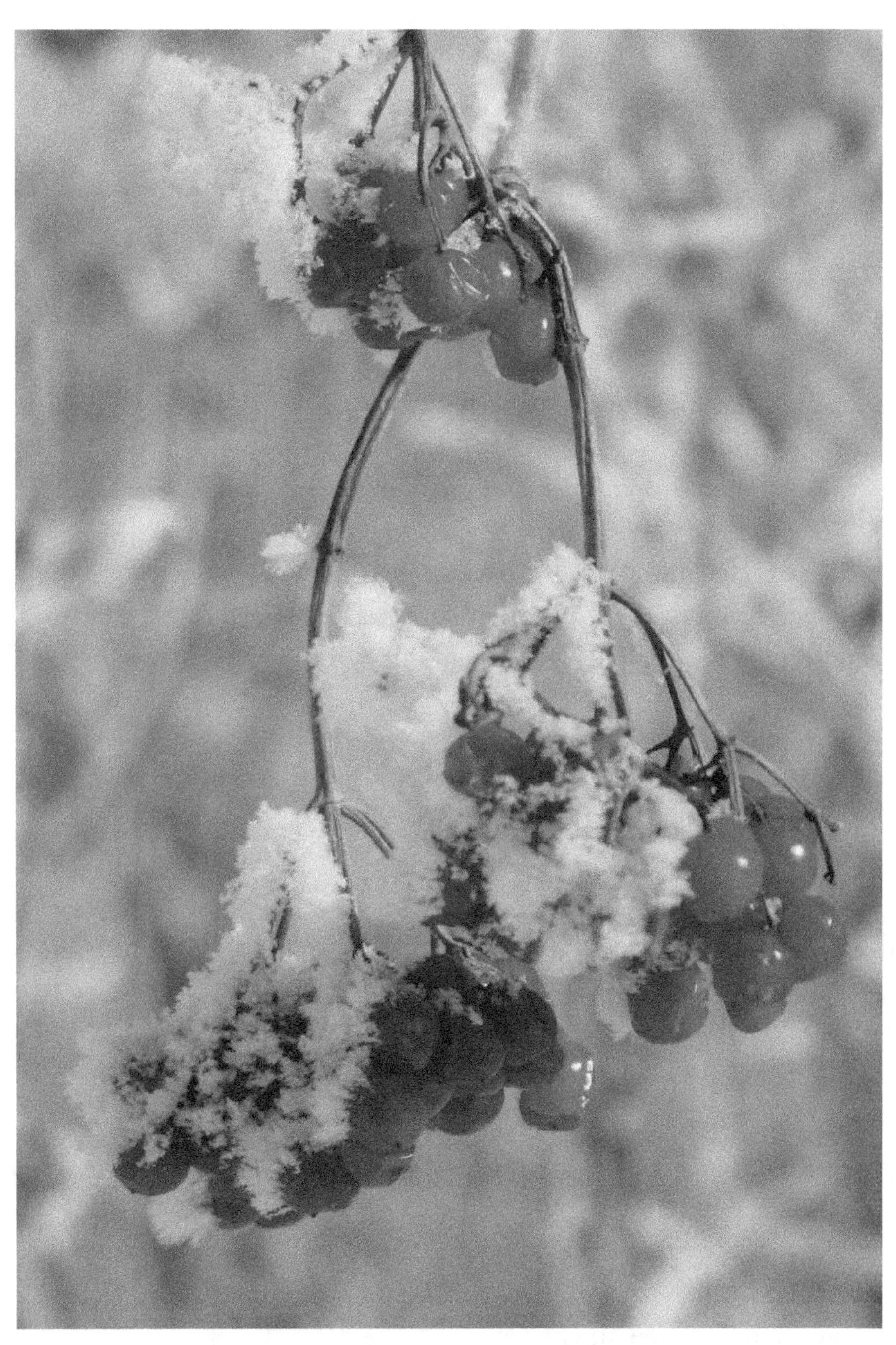

January Berries

Curt Liesveld

Notes toward a prairie paleontology

Chuck Peek

Suppose a yellow bus, possibly lost,
and in it us, suspended
in some willing amber drop of disbelief,

from which, extracted and strewn like a skeleton
across the makeshift museum of another summer,
we, too, are reconvened by Eiseley's of a later day.

One figures that our books
must have helped us map our way up
from marshes of facts

toward at least a toe-hold
on all the destinies on which we stand,
another guessing our opposable tongues

allowed us to converse not only with ourselves
but with the beings in the bags of fossils
we carried with us like ancients their household gods.

Still another suggesting that the eye
at the center of our memory
must have allowed us to see downriver

as sacked corn disappeared in puffs of smoke,
horses captured villages,
as rain from Spain fell mainly on our plain.

This much by then might be elementary.
Red clouds can roll and uncommon buffalo thunder
even in absentia.

But when they had so assembled us,
could they have inferred we had the faculty
to fathom where the animals first named the tribes?

Reason sufficient to reconstruct
the dizzying leap from suicide to birth,
from white man's three to Whitman's four?

When everywhere became here, could they discern
in red brick walls or yellow brick roads
or even in our accumulated dust

how our Dorothy's felt beckoned to more distant dreams,
still found some power to believe
in what lies a long moment hidden by the prairie moon?

He Knew What Love Was

Judy Lorenzen

Leathered skin, pock-marked;
he was 38 with sad green eyes.
he raised his hand in life-skills class
answered the question: What is love?
Said he hadn't known love, except one time.
The oldest in a family of boys,
beat every daybreak and sunset by his raging father
who'd come into his room, vodka gripped in one hand,
he'd punch him in his bed, then on the floor,
against the dresser and wall—
maybe punch him for picking up his fork wrong, or some such crime.
By 7th grade, he ached to get his beatings over with.
Hate was devoured and drunk in his home—
he could give plenty of examples of hate—
the brothers never spoke—ever—
the only sure thing in his life.

At 16 he was sentenced to the penitentiary.
In prison, he got word his old man died drunk in a car wreck.
Said he felt nothing—just nothing—wished he could.
Twenty-six—set for release
Brother Jimmie wrote a letter,
he was coming for him.
Jimmie picked him up on South 14th Street in Lincoln—
drove 90 miles to the old trailer park—

windows busted out,
weeds tall around the trailer,
his old rusted Chevy pickup
still out in the trees.

He and Jimmie started drinking vodka.
Their words spilled easy, smooth as vodka goes down.
He felt happy for the first time in his life—really happy.
They sat in that old red Chevy,
watched the orange sun dip down below old cottonwood branches,
spoke of Daddy—and cried about why Mama left…
Then Jimmie turned the ignition—
that old truck fired up.
Jimmie rammed it into the cottonwood again and again and again.
They laughed and laughed like they had never laughed before.
Jimmie pissed himself—and they laughed even harder.
Said he knew what love felt like once,
and said he'd never forget.

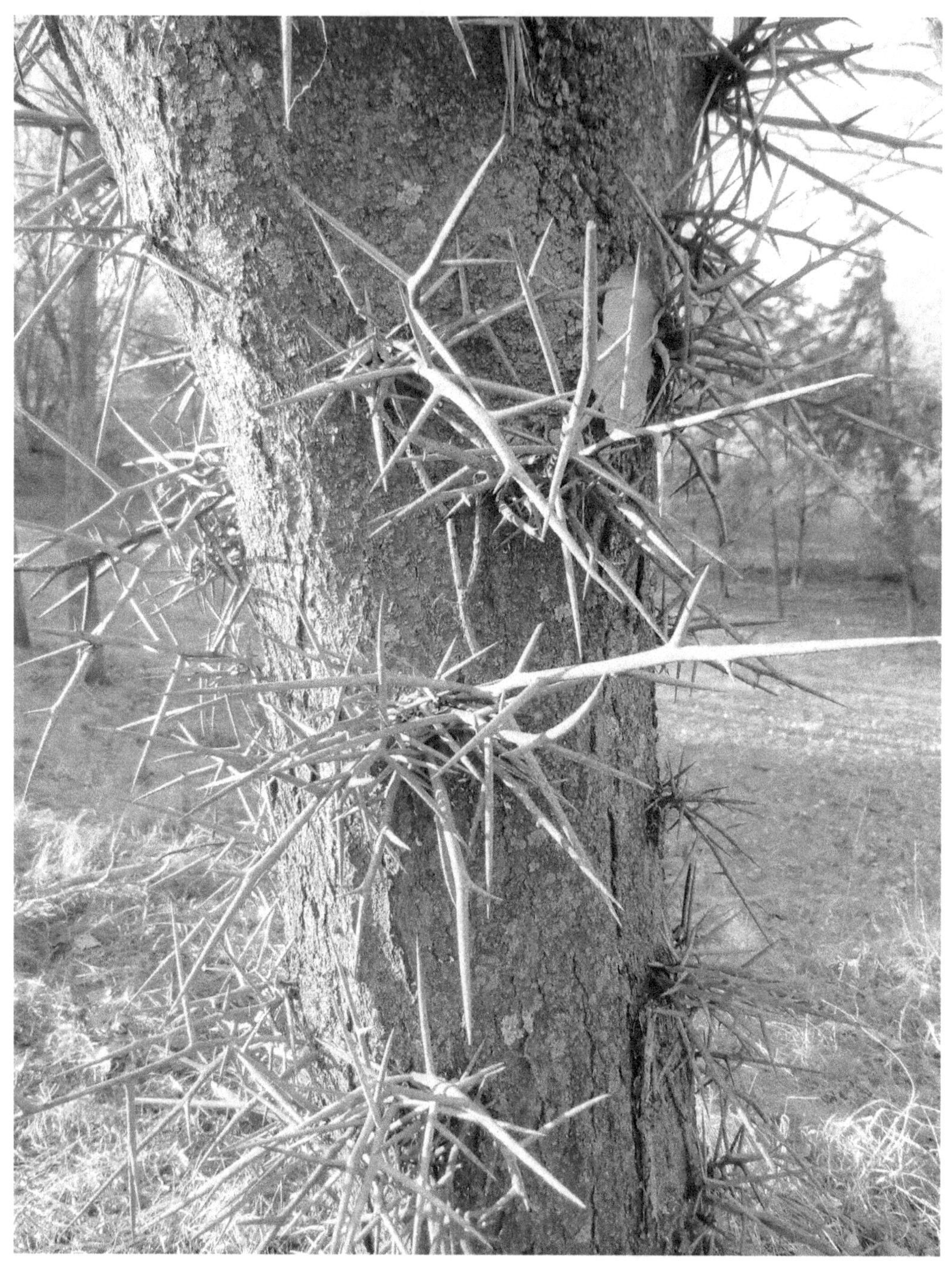

Locust Thorns

Robert Ericson

Love Stuff

Ally Halley

She was humming and up to her elbows in flour. She was humming the instrumental intro to Metallica's "Enter Sandman." The rhythm was conducive to vigorous kneading. Plus, she liked the contrast between the wholesome act of making bread and the raw vitriol of the heavy metal single. She could feel the fatigue in her shoulders, and the yeasty mound in her hands was pushing back; it was almost ready.

"Watcha makin', Grandma?" a small voice asked.

Jeanne looked down at the pair of brown eyes and sandy bangs gazing at her over the other side of the countertop, "Baguettes to go with the lasagna for supper."

"Can I help?"

"Sure, Kai. You can tell me if it's done kneading. Grab the stool."

The boy's eyes became saucers of excitement, and he disappeared to find the step stool. With its assistance, the countertop was now at waist height for him. His eager eyes locked onto his grandma and his little hands milked the air in anticipation. Although he was proud to have just turned six, he was the youngest of three brothers and small for his age. Today though, it was just Kai and Grandma; he didn't have to share. He watched in fascination as Jeanne massaged the dough. "It looks done to me, Grandma. Let's bake it!"

Jeanne laughed, "Not yet, we have to test it." She pulled off two small hunks of dough and handed one to Kai. "Now, roll it into a ball between your hands like Play-doh."

Kai rolled his ball with comical intensity. "Done," he announced.

Jeanne nodded in approval. "Beautiful. Now watch what I do with mine. See how I carefully pull and stretch it out into a circle?"

"Like this?"

"Perfect! Just a little more gently. Okay, now if we can stretch it out so thin that you can almost see through it, it's done. If it tears, I have to knead it more."

Kai's forehead knitted in concentration; he wanted to impress Grandma. He held his disk of dough up to the light, trying to see through it. "Is this thin enough, Grandma?"

"Beautiful! Ready to shape them?" Jeanne reached to take Kai's dough ball when she saw him take a deep, convulsive breath. Even though she saw it coming, she didn't react quickly enough and caught the full brunt of Kai's sneeze. The little dough ball was saturated.

Kai was horrified. "I'm sorry, Grandma!"

Jeanne blinked and stifled a laugh. "It's okay. Just try to cover your mouth next time. We'll throw that ball away. Let's wash our hands."

After their little mishap, Jeanne cut the remaining dough in half and showed Kai how to shape his half. Soon, they had one baguette and one slightly bumpy baguette set aside to rise. Jeanne hung up her apron and wiped down the countertop.

"That was fun! Now you know how to make bread! Your brothers don't even know how to do that."

At the mention of his brothers, Kai's smile faded and his head dropped. "They're going to make fun of me."

Dismayed at the sudden change in Kai's demeanor, Jeanne bent down to hug her grandson. "Why would they make fun of you?"

"Because cooking is girl stuff, and I'm a *boy*."

Jeanne smiled and released a breath she didn't realize she was holding. "Oh, honey, cooking isn't girl stuff."

He sniffed. "It's not?"

"Of course it's not."

She watched his little brain trying to puzzle it out. He wiped his nose with the back of his hand. "What is it?"

"Cooking is *love* stuff."

"Love stuff?"

"Yeah, *love* stuff." Jeanne hugged Kai a little tighter. "Cooking is hard. Cooking takes time. When you take the time to cook for someone, you're not just taking care of them by giving them healthy food, you're giving them a gift of yourself; a gift of your time. You know what I mean?"

Kai heaved a shuttering sigh, "So, the bread we made shows our family we love them?"

Jeanne smiled. "Yep. Everything we cook has a little love baked into it. That's what makes it taste so good."

Kai looked at the pair of baguettes on the countertop and grinned. "Can we make the lasagna now?"

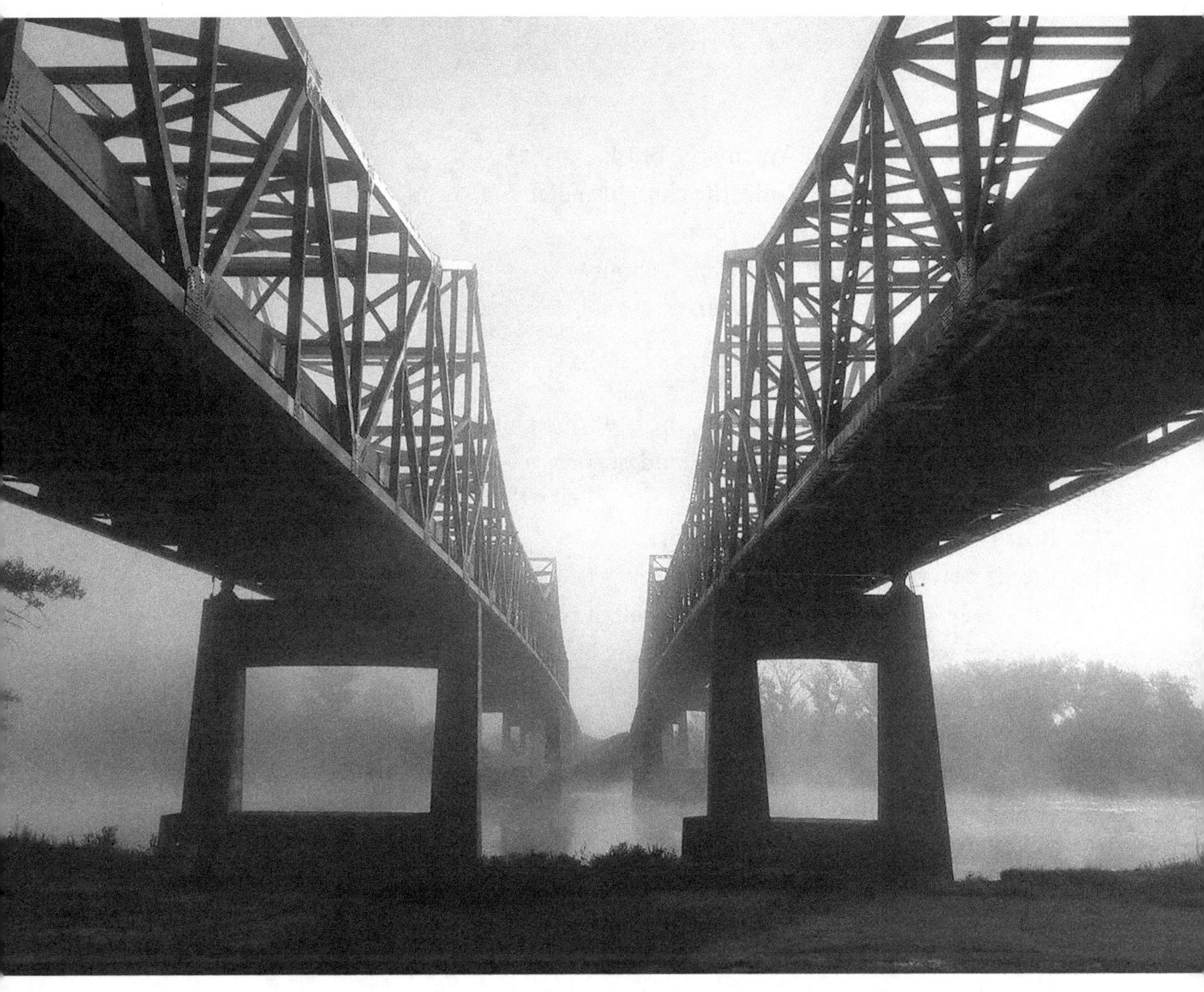

Mormon Bridge at Dawn

Julian Adair

Lunch Stop on the Bike Tour

Lucy Adkins

It was a little café bar in Worms, Nebraska,
yes, Worms, W O R M S, like the churchly edict
written in 1521, the Diet of Worms,
and that was another thing to laugh about
because it was a café; it was a bar,
and besides the menu of worms,
there was a faded hamburger on the sign
and a glass of Coke, and Hamms, the beer refreshing—
the land of sky blue waters in the land of corn.

It was late June, the middle of the prairie,
the air heavy with the thick pollen scent of corn,
the steady-sure, indolent, growing smell of corn,
and now with the Tour, there were eighty bicycles
parked out front of the café bar,
sag wagons, and inside eighty riders.

And when the old man pulled up in his pickup truck,
got out for his midday meal—
old man in his old man overalls,
hot, bare-armed, peace-loving, whiskered old man—
when he got out of his truck and saw
the eighty bicycles, he knew that lunch would be late
that day, and the waitress in the blue dress
harried and flying about.

But he got out of his truck anyway,
got out and reached open the door
and there were the eighty riders
in a rainbow of different colored jerseys:
orange and blue, mint green, yellow,
three shades of purple, yellow-orange, gold—
muscle-calved men,
tight black pants on their tight behinds,
eating up the hamburgers,
drinking up the Hamms.

Well, shit-fire, he said.
They could have been his grandsons,
they could have been his kids,
taking over the way they do;
and now here, too, in Worms, Nebraska
where you think you can count
on a simple thing like a little quiet, a burger,
a small glass of beer on a hot June day.

Mormon Wife

Barbara Salvatore

SOCKS

Dora watched everything, her dark glassy eyes reflecting everything around her. She could see through people but not into them. Like a crow, she perched, always warning of impending danger, long before anyone saw it coming. Magghie ruffled Dora's feathers the moment she first laid her black eyes on Magghie. It was Magghie's beauty that was so threatening. It was a beauty completely unaware of itself, or the power that it potentially held. Perhaps it was the German chamomile teas that Magghie drank that made her skin glow. Perhaps it was the lack of self-consciousness that came from never looking at herself in a glass. Perhaps it was the way she sang from the time she awoke, and throughout her day's menial chores and wanderings. Perhaps it was her eyes that looked until they were done looking, without ever thinking she needed permission.

Or perhaps it was her ease of moving, over ground, up on a high horse, or wagon seat, through the woods, up a tree, at the butter churn, in the garden. Perhaps it was all of these things that made her so attractive. But Dora knew, truly it was the girl's eyes. She knew her husband could not even look into them, without blushing to his brows, giving himself away, though he continually pretended his attentions went unnoticed. *She* knew. *She* knew what was beautiful. She also knew that she herself was not. But the walls that she closed in around her, against that suffocating winter, protected her little against the blossoming she would bear witness to that spring. She *knew* the girl would further bloom, and blood would begin to rise, and those blue eyes would continue to melt men. The madness took over till she could not put her head down to a full night's sleep, in that cabin, in that bed, in that valley, any more. Each night, sleep came shorter and more frequently disturbed by the waking, ravenous child within her and her own haunting dreams. No, she could not rely on sleep. And she could not rely on *him*. She felt him pull away, as she shrank, and her belly grew, and *she knew,* it was just a matter of time before he would turn against her. Dora dreaded it and so planned her escape—back to the civilized life that she once had. Back to safe traditions, back to embroidering.

So, she planned it, in the middle of the night, while quietly knitting extra warm socks for her journey. She would not rely on him, or anyone to get her there. She would not rely on that monstrous wagon. She would walk back there herself, on her own two feet, carrying her own precious baby. She would walk but she would not wear out her feet. Waiting for the ground to thaw, that long month before spring, she knit twenty-seven pairs of socks before she stopped.

25 Years

Linda Robinson

How fast can 25 years go?
I guess I can say I don't care or don't know.
But I know that it's long enough to get children raised,
to weather life's storms and to come out unphased.
To have felt all the feelings this world presents
and arise from the rubble with most of my sense.
To know that pure joy is like liquid gold
as it seeps through your fingers just too hard to hold.
To know seconds and minutes snowball into years,
picking up laughter and sadness and tears.
Like a breeze and a blink or a breath and a sigh
every day was a year that turned into goodbye.
But to know every sunrise and set was a blessing,
like God reached down and I felt his caressing.
More precious than silver were these years spent.
I just wish I knew where all the time went.
Every day I would wait for the future to start
while I tucked every memory deep in my heart.
Like a butterfly born to flutter away,
25 years was just part of today.

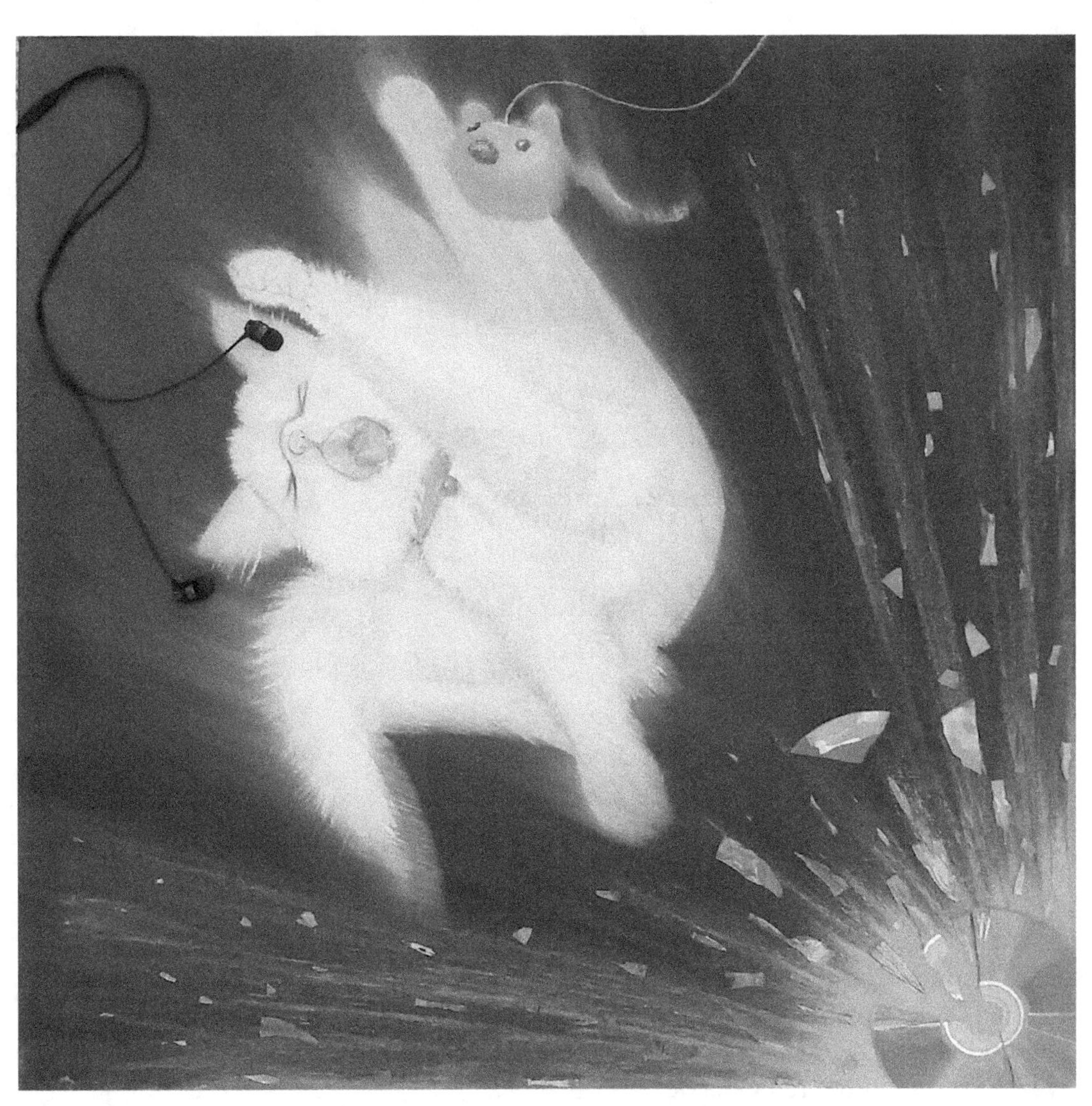

Rockin' Louie

Lila Rose

Nebraska Road Trip with Tom Waits

Amy Plettner

Highway sixty-six, Sunday, early morn,
churches still dark, steeples shrouded with fog.

Streetlights flash yellow. We take no caution,
whiskey gone from our breath,

headed west into a thick drizzle. It's April,
a Christmas star atop the grain elevators,

corn the true Savior, and the path to salvation is
an iron rail guiding us past Tuxedo Park,

Avengers playing at the Isis Theatre,
and every hour's happy hour at the *Someplace Else* bar.

The streets all have names that sound like rednecks,
and I'm still living on the alimony.

You're wearing your wedding ring,
cut diamonds and garnets in a swirl of silver-gold .

You find your way beneath my skirt.
We're cruising in the red Galaxie.

I close my eyes, move to the slap of wipers,
the rain getting harder.

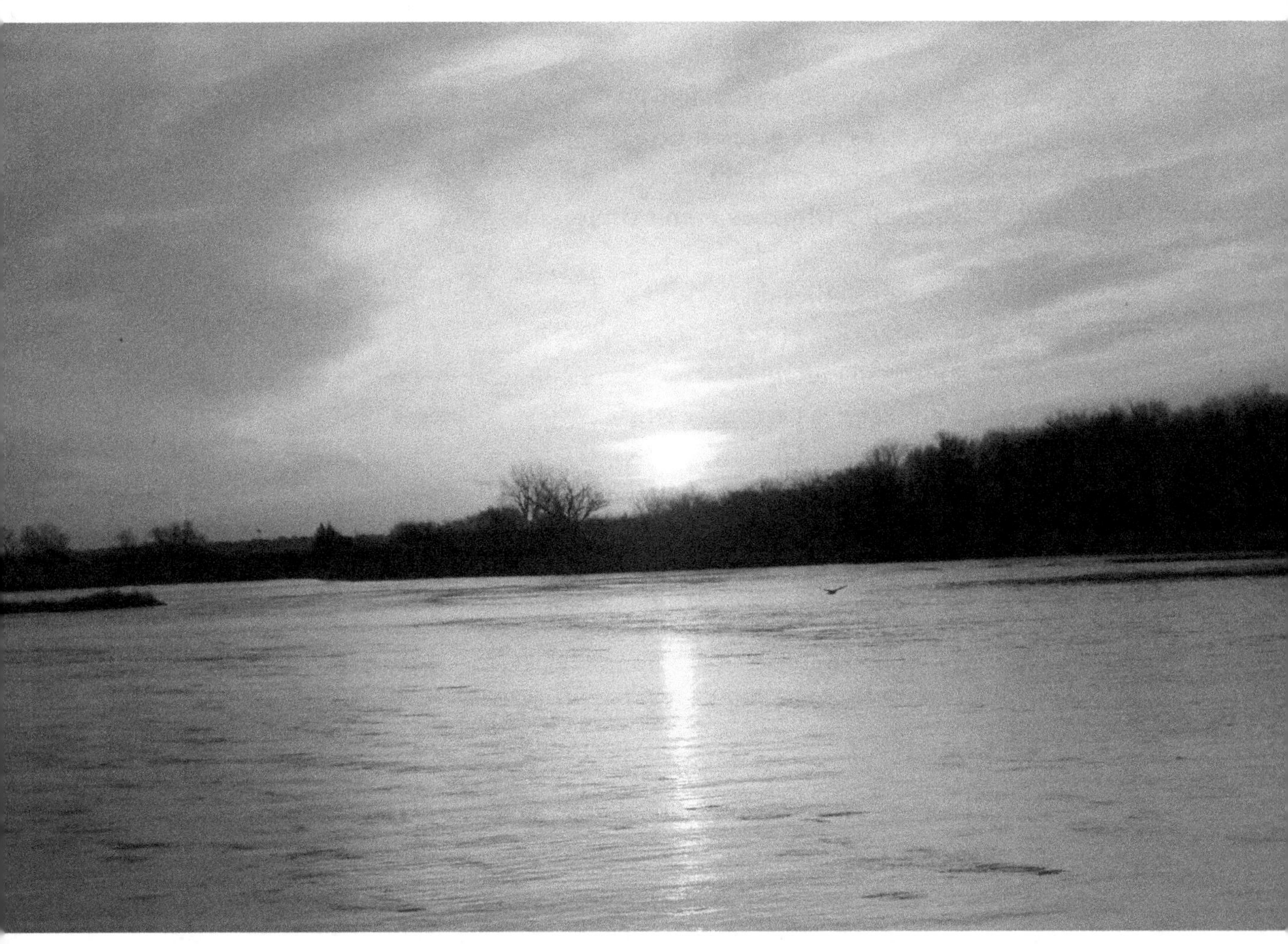

Nebraska Sunset

Chris Richter

Bully

Gracie Ellis

How could you?
How could you kill someone so much inside?
That they cry as soon as they get home
That they wish they were dead right now
That they are wondering why they even exist right now?

They act like it doesn't bother them
That they are strong
But trust me, it hurts so much
How could you do that to a person?
Honestly, I don't understand it
How could you destroy somebody's light in their eye?
How could you even live with yourself?
Knowing that you did that to someone just with your words.

I wouldn't want you going home
Thinking that you don't deserve to be here.
Words hurt
So please think before you speak.
You matter and so does that person you bullied
Just remember words are the cruelest things in the world

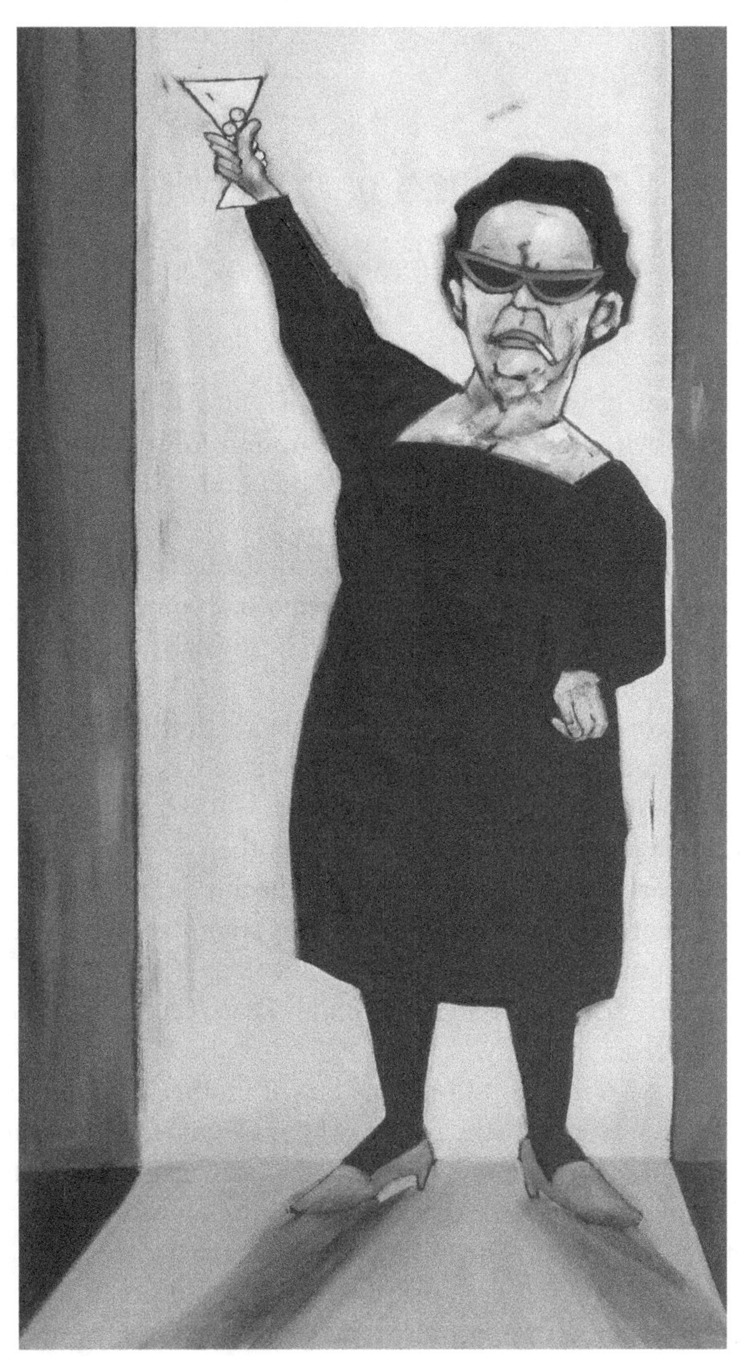

A Martini and a Cigarette

Paula Wallace

Not Ready to Wake

Bridgit Kuenning-Pollpeter

We sit on the couch, worn and dirty from life, next to Ross who slumbers as a black-and-white movie hums softly in the background. Your hands folded against me as if in prayer; your tiny bulk nestled into my body, and we are like a family. Mother, father, baby—but you are not mine.

I hold you, Penny, in my arms, sweeping away the fears that wake you. Sniffling, unsure of where you are, you see me and stretch out your little arms. I stroke the downy, dark hair that grows longer each day. Your tiny baby fist rubs sleep from your eyes, still you yawn, not ready to wake.

Related, we are connected biologically, but you are not my daughter. You are our niece by birth, but you have become so much more.

My heart stretches towards yours, longing to know this feeling always. You breathe steady, slowly, surely, and for a moment, I am a mother.

I imagine us as part of a holiday snow globe as the three of us lounge on the couch at two o'clock in the morning. The mist of this fantasy shimmers around us, engulfing us in warmth. The rhythm of your soft snoring strides along with the beating of my heart.

How long have my arms ached to hold a child? I can feel the emptiness of my baby whose life drained from my body.

We were proud, we were happy. I felt the kiss of motherhood, but the kiss turned cold. On my twenty-seventh birthday, my baby was wrenched from my womb. My tears swallowed me as I sat on Ross's lap shivering, convulsing, trying to understand. He held me tight, hushing and rocking, his tears mingling with mine.

One, two, three doctors explained how the permanent damage to my body—an elevated heart rate, low blood pressure, diabetes—would break me if a child grew inside me; if I could even sustain you. Next came the news of my inhospitable womb. Even without underlying health issues threatening to squash any pregnancy, fertility problems would be a plague. Ross and I walked hand-in-hand silently out of the doctor's office, the only warmth coming from his hand.

The burden of heartache grew solid around me. Once again, tears streaked my wooden face. My heart stopped. Unable to navigate this storm, we nailed the shutters closed.

Ross sustained me through the hurricane that left us weak, homeless but standing. In each other, we found a sliver of joy. We rebuilt our life, picking through the fragments. Strength came in silence, hope, love. Together we stood, in sickness and in health, 'til-death-do-us-part.

Stroking my skin gently, melting the ice from my lips, plucking my body ripened and firm, he whispered desire back into me. Once again, I recognized the yearning for touch. Restless, eager, I breathed him in.

I held strength renewed and fresh, but longing seeped into every aspect of life. My dream, my hope to call a child mine, was never out of reach. Every turn, every encounter picked the healing scab away.

The pregnant women on the bus, complaining of aches and pains that I would never experience. The mothers at the park swinging giggling children, pushing chattering babies in their jogging strollers. Rain soaked the land, smudging the landscape into a blurred image.

It was Mother's Day. A day celebrating motherhood; a joy I did not know. My great-grandmother bore nine children. My grandmother birthed five babies. My mother gave birth to four beautiful children. My sister, two years younger, had two kids. I alone stood barren.

It was a spring day warm and balmy. The men stood around the grill, taking turns explaining the best way to grill burgers and brats. The women set out the food; arranging the table. Children scampered—weaving in and out of the adult activity.

We sat, relaxed and full of good living. Presents distributed among the mothers.

"We thank everyone for coming today," my sister, Brook, spoke. "We also want to congratulate Matt and Christina on their pregnancy."

The room overflowed with congratulatory shouts as my sister broke the news about her brother-in-law and his wife. I smiled, hugging the happy couple as thoughts stormed against my heart.

"We also want to tell you guys—Brook is pregnant again too," Brook's husband announced.

Gasps and, "You're joking, right?" flooded the room.

"Nope, we're really pregnant again," Brook replied.

I stood, pushing my sunglasses down on my face. "Excuse me," I mumbled as I rushed to the bathroom.

Sitting on the seat of the toilet, I choked, unable to breathe. Slamming my hands into my eyes, I tried to stop the tears. Stars burst in my vision as a wet trickle escaped down my cold cheek. Placing a hand on my flat stomach, the emptiness engulfed me.

Needles pricked my body, spreading head-to-feet. A pain sharp and hot.

Ross knocked softly on the door. "Baby, are you okay?"

Opening the door, he slid in, placing his arms around me.

"I knew you were upset," he said.

I smashed my face into his shoulder as though I could enter his body, be a part of his being. A choked, dying sound poured from my throat. My chest heaved as I struggled to find breath. I couldn't speak. This was my fate.

Ross stroked my hair and held me tight. His quiet sniffles joined mine swelling into an inharmonious chorus.

I thought of the long days, months, weeks, years weaving around and around, taunting me, blaming me. I was not a woman; I could not bring life to an empty, barren land.

A year later, I once again faced the confession of a woman's pregnancy.

It was cold and rainy. It was April, warm, but stormy. A season for childbearing; a day for bad news.

My youngest sister, Rachel, sat in my living room, quiet. I sat at the kitchen table, popping almonds into my mouth, enjoying the salty goodness.

Rachel sat at our computer working last minute on homework.

My mother spoke as Ross emerged from the back of our flat. "Well, Rachel has something to tell you."

"What, are you getting married?" I joked.

Rachel sat facing the computer monitor as she said, "Uh—yeah, but also I'm having a baby."

My hand stopped half way between the tin can and my mouth. Thoughts bounced through my head as I tried to speak. An image of Rachel as a chubby red baby, bald with bright blue eyes, flashed through my mind.

This was my little sister, not even out of high school yet and now thrown into adulthood with one action. Weeks of dating resulting in parenthood. How did my mother feel about this? How did Rachel feel? What should I say?

Ross saved me by congratulating Rachel.

"Do you plan on keeping the baby?" I asked, regretting the words.

"Yes. If I'm going through nine months of this then I'm keeping it."

"Well congratulations," I said, hugging my eighteen-year-old sister.

Nine months later, I stood, holding you, Penny. I was detached, unwilling to shatter again. You were wrapped tightly in a blanket, a gift, but not for me. I passed you back to my little sister and her boy-husband, wondering why the world had shifted.

You are almost one-year-old now. A well-fed belly protrudes out, and dimples speckle your legs and thighs. Your petite hands and feet move and kick and reach and grab. The world is interesting and full of excitement.

I stand in the bathroom cleaning, and I hear you chugging around the corner, curious of my whereabouts. Holding onto the doorframe, you stand. I stretch my arms towards you, ready to pick you up, but you are quick.

I hear the beating of my heart as you take three steps into my arms. One, two, three. Your first independent steps are taken for me. For me; your shadow mother. I cradle you as you make soft plopping noises with your mouth.

I am proud. We cheer as we go to tell Ross about this new feat, but I realize this is all fleeting for me. You will go home with your real mommy and daddy, and we will be left alone, hearing the echoes of your voice as we try to stifle it with sound. Music, television, books, computer, we attempt to fill the cavern, but you are in our hearts, our being.

Tonight you, Penny, are mine, ours. Our heat combines incubating you as you sleep tucked against my torso and chest. Your weight in my arms fills my heart. You move your head up as though looking at me, but you remain asleep. Resting your head on my chest, sure of where you are, sure of who I am, you sigh, content—and I am content.

I lay back against Ross feeling exhaustion sweep over me. I won't let you go though.

Later Ross will carry both of us into bed. Snuggled between us, you seem so small. I dream of holding you every night.

On either side of you, we protect you. I kiss your soft skin made golden by the summer sun, like me. For now, you are mine, I am your mother.

Ross reaches out to grab my hand. "I love you."

In this moment, we are one; we are a family. In this moment, we embrace this dream. In this moment, we are not ready to wake.

Pricksong

Marilyn June Coffey

I am cursed
by a large penis
which I planted in a flower pot
in my living room.
When it grew, like a cactus,
it looked thirsty and,
being kindly at heart,
I allayed its thirst
with water. It sprouted wings.
Now it flies around the house
and sings at me.
Once I tried to shoot it down
but horrified, it shriveled up
into a ball, retracting everything
it had ever said to me. What
could I do? I didn't have the heart
to follow through. Now it tries to get
in bed with me. I am afraid.
It is so big. It looks so thirsty.
It is never satisfied. Last night
when I pushed it back, it cried.

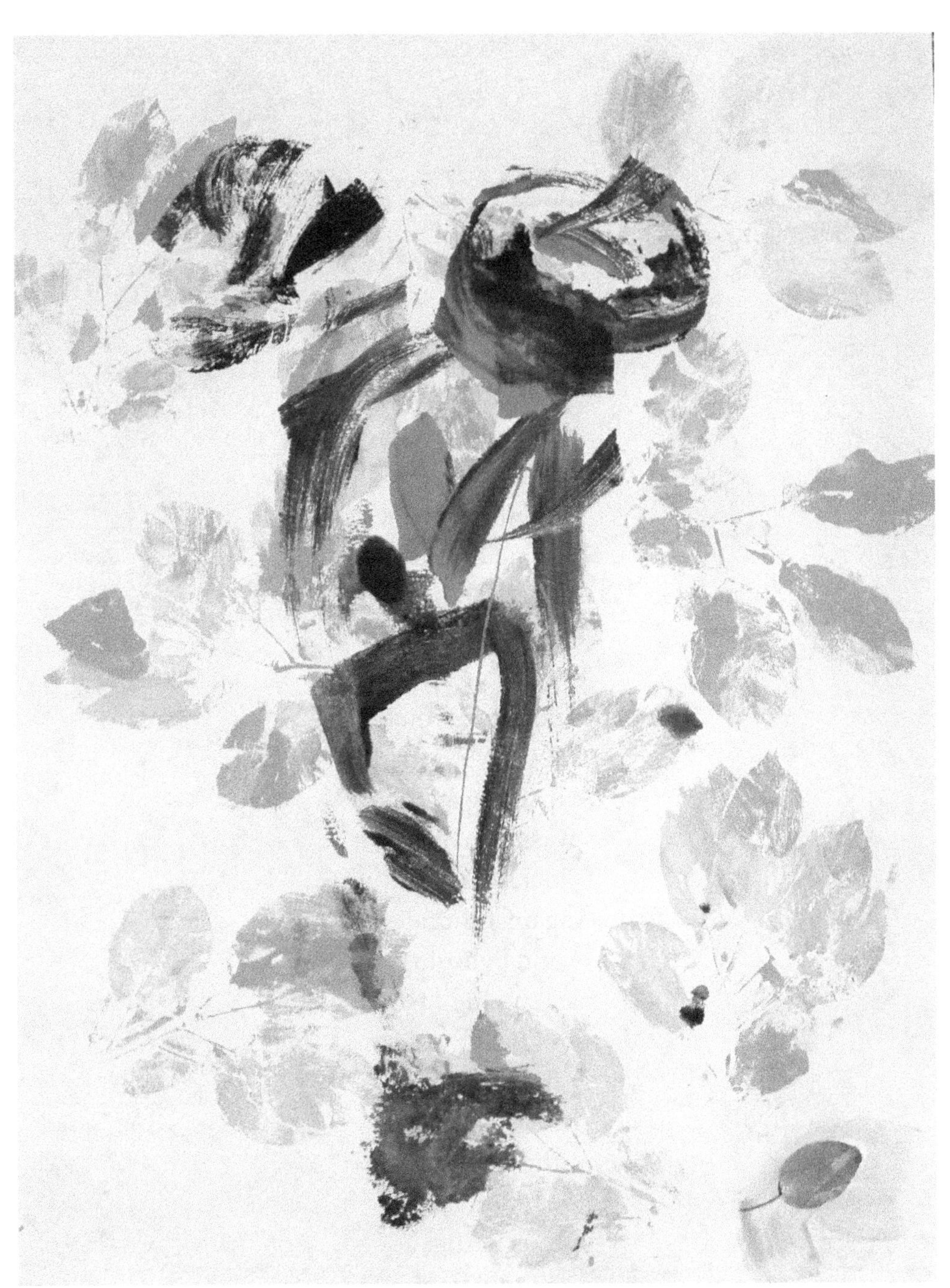

Mother Art

Sally Deskins

Rain Crow

Marilyn Dorf

All afternoon
the rain crow,
feeling the rise
and the fall of a
barometer he does
not even own,
sits on a branch
of the cottonwood
predicting, predicting.
And Ol' Mr. Morrie,
expecting a gully-
washer, believes,
locks his doors
against thunder
and lightning,
hail and high wind,
looking to waken
floating down
the Mississippi,
the rain crow,
still on duty,
echoing,
I told you!
I told you!

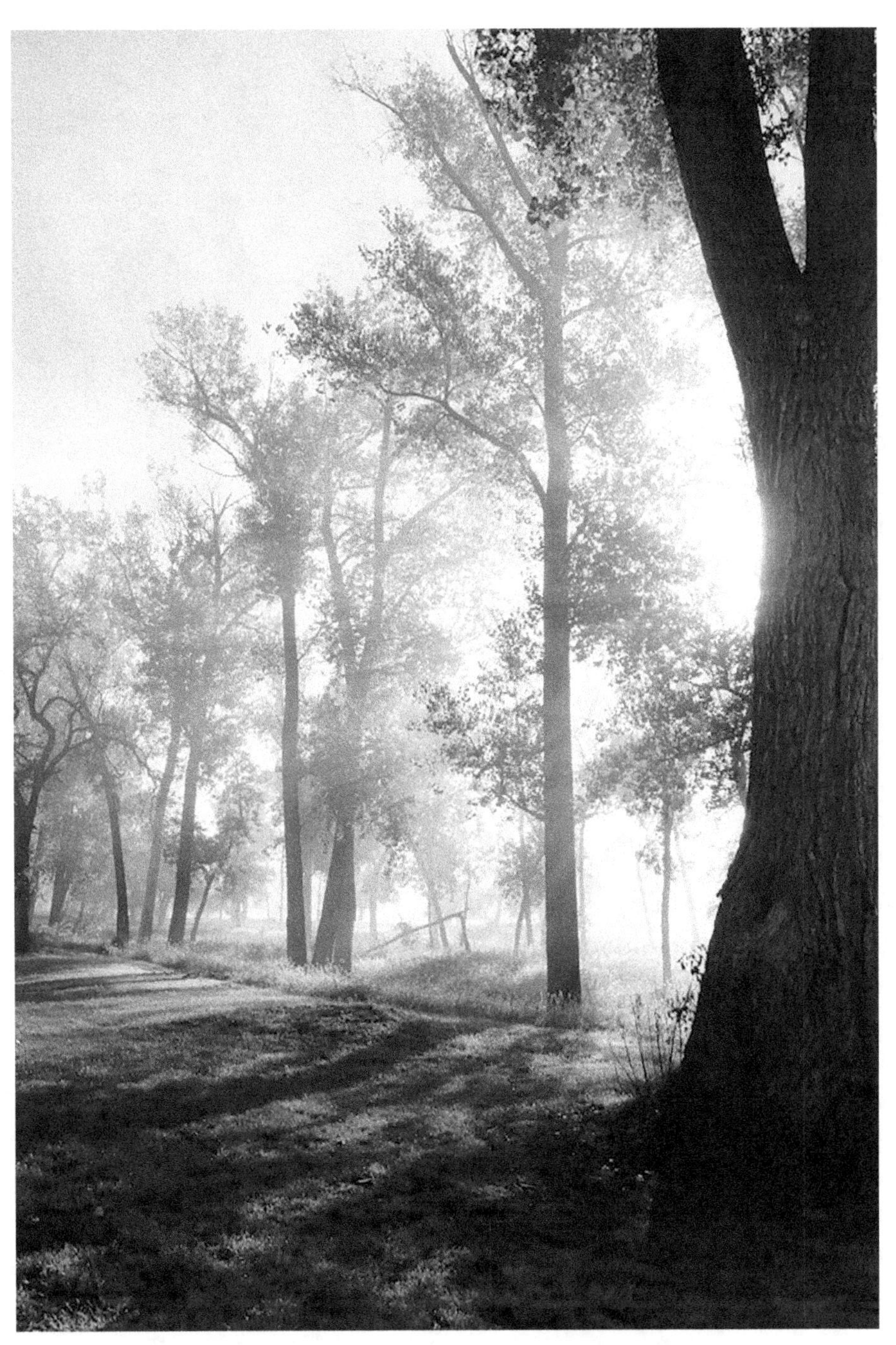

Dawn at Dodge Park

Julian Adair

Escape

Michael Skau

Back in fourth grade, Carol Harper would chase
me home from school and try to kiss
me. Years have passed since then. I remember though
that I used to run the two short blocks
home, planning alternate routes to take in case
she waited ahead, that naughty miss
I was fully prepared in boyish years to go
to any length then to outfox.

She caught me once: it was not unpleasant, but
I pretended it was. Now in my house
I sit with balding pate and wrinkled brow
and liver spots and swollen gut,
too young to die and too old to carouse.
Carol Harper, where are you now?

Saying Good-Bye to His Melancholy

Amy Plettner

I talk to myself,
don't take him personally.
I don't listen,
get angry, and flip him the bird.

He doesn't like identifying
anything with wings,
and my days are full
of kestrel, quail, killdeer,

on this crease of marriage
where miracles of flight are pressed down,
and the vows that moved across my lips
didn't say anything about being your mother.

I am angry. I won't remind you
to brush your teeth before bed
or change your underwear.

You tell me, *take it easy* in bed.
I say, *leave, unhook your suffering*
from my winged hips.

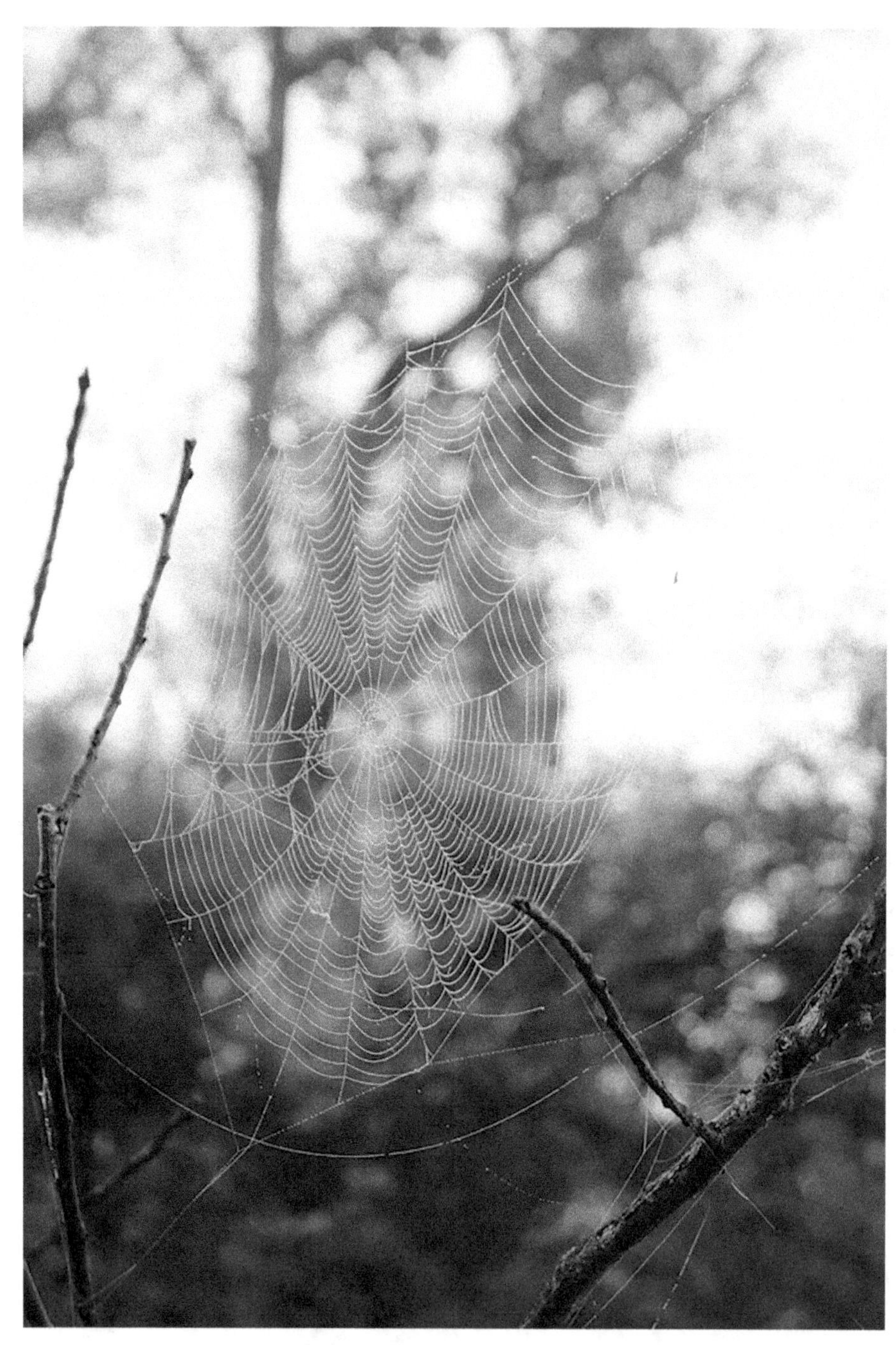

Spider Web

Julian Adair

Spike

Karen Heckman Stork

Remember the summer you were six years old
and you caught a caterpillar in a Mason jar,
you added a stick and some leaves to keep it alive
and you punched holes in the lid so it could breathe,
and then you sat and sat and watched it for hours?

Remember how surprised you were when the green
bumpy bug started spinning itself into a
mummy-like gray cocoon attached to that stick
and you asked how could it stay alive inside
and how could it eat, and you kept it by your bed at night?

Remember how an orange-black butterfly emerged
covered with drops of wetness and bits of gray cocoon
clinging to its body, struggling to open its wings
which seemed stuck together like thin strips of Velcro,
and you exclaimed, "It's alive!"?

Remember how you opened the lid and the orange-black
Monarch flew up and landed on your left shoulder
and we could hardly see it because it matched your orange blouse,
and how still you stood as it explored your shoulder and
finally opened its wings like a prisoner flexing new-found freedom?

Remember how you christened him "Spike" and we all watched
him take off from your shoulder, and we chased him across
the field next to our house, and how he got smaller and smaller,
and finally, was only an orange-black speck in the sky?

There's a mountain in Mexico where these
orange-black former prisoners gather in huge numbers.
I hope Spike found his way home.

Photograph of a Gathering

Greg Kosmicki

I recognize my Grandfather Munger
and Grandmother; Uncle Ralph, maybe age
five or six, no others. They all look like
desperadoes from some western movie—
drooping moustaches, women's hair pulled back.
Some of them actually smiling. No one
knows, anymore, where this picture, taken
at some sort of gathering, in front
of a sod house, was shot. Schoolhouse or church,
or one of my ancestor's first prairie
homes, one of their neighbor's? We'll never know.

When Mom died three summers ago, she lived
most of the time in her mind in a place
like this, if not this house. She talked about
Granddad going to Ogallala for
thirty horses. Then she asked about our
daughter's test scores, chided my fifty-year-
old sister for going out after dark
because she's just a little girl. Ten years
ago, maybe fifteen, she could have put
a name to every face in that picture
except maybe a hired hand or two.

Now, there's no one in the world but
me, and maybe a couple cousins on
my mom's side, who can recognize any
face in that picture, and when we die, no
face will be known, or if they are known, we
do not know who the person is, who knows.
Maybe one of the neighbors from 60
years ago has a grandkid still alive
who could look at that picture and see great
uncle Alexander or Grandma Anne
but that link has been broken. The picture
is in a box in my basement. No one
will recognize these faces, sad sod house.
It's that simple. It has happened again.

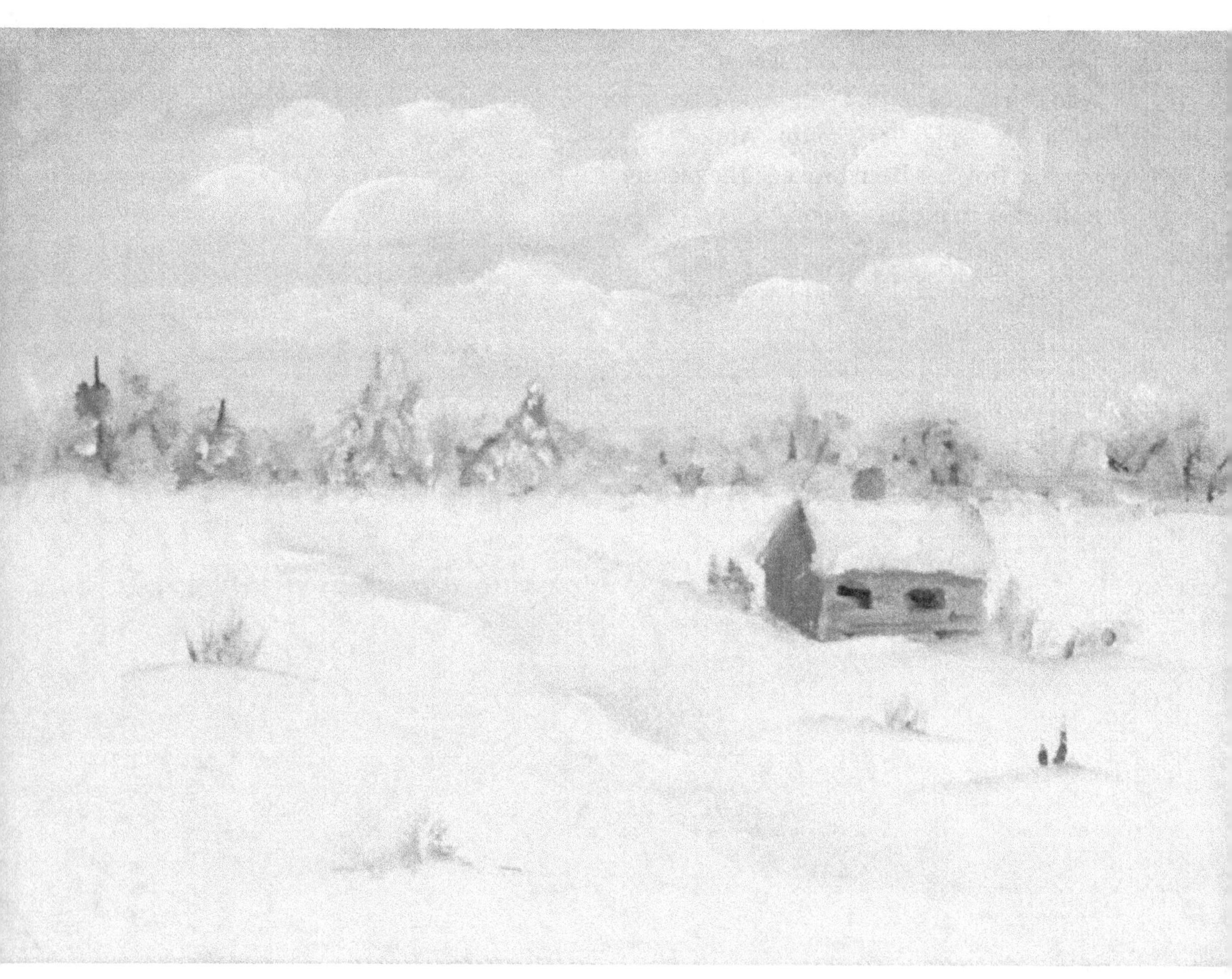

Winter Landscape

LaVetta Vamosi

A Pitstop

Justin Kruse

Tony had an apartment lined up for the summer, but toward the end of finals week he made the decision to go home, or rather, to his parent's home for a few days. He was, after all, already moved in. His parents would be happy to see him, yes, but really he just wanted to bathe in the comfort of childhood familiarity.

Tony hadn't been home for more than a night in probably two years. Much as he loved his parents, they were from a time far removed from modern society, and they had trouble relating. He remembered the route though. Always the same two-lane roads and through the same tiny towns. The roads with no shoulder that dip into a drainage ditch without warning. With tar patches every few feet to remind you that the concrete hasn't been replaced in a couple decades. The towns with crumbling brick storefronts lining the main street, a grain elevator visible a few blocks behind them, and a row of pickup trucks parked out in front of the lone bar. Tony may have lived in a city for the last few years, but that setting still meant home to him.

Of course he had that one last final on Friday afternoon before he could leave, and that meant a night drive. Inevitably, he had to stop for gas along the way.

In one of those little nameless towns is a smallish gas station that sits somewhat away from the rest of the community. It's easily accessible from the highway of course, but nearly what you would consider out of town. It has older pumps with no card swipe, so you have to pay inside. The building is just large enough to accommodate a cashier's counter with a rack of cigarettes, a couple rows of snacks, and a refrigerated area with your favorite soft drinks and lite beers. Tony had used that station maybe once before, but on this trip he was sinking below a quarter tank as he passed through, so the presence of that station seemed almost fortunate.

As anywhere else, he pulled up to a pump, got the fuel flowing, checked the pump number so he could tell the cashier, and leaned up against the car.

Now, most gas stations have a bathroom, and that old place was no exception. The difference was that this one was only accessible from the outside. Tony found himself staring at the restroom door as he waited for the pump to kick off.

Ordinarily you would have to ask the attendant on duty for a key to open it, but Tony noticed that the door had been left slightly ajar. He made a mental note to let the cashier know when he paid for the gas.

He knew filling the tank would take some time, but waited patiently, listening to the sound of gasoline flowing through the nozzle and feeling the car settle slightly as it became heavier. He glanced at other cars zipping past on the highway and wondered which ones would stop there before he left, or which ones were from his home county. Every time his eyes passed over that restroom door it seemed to have opened just a bit more. At first, he could just tell that it was open, but each time he looked back the black gap widened. No light glared from within, just a line of deep darkness around the door.

As Tony stared it down, it slowly, quietly creaked open the rest of the way. Clearly it was the wind, catching a big metal sail and pulling it along. A wind that Tony neither felt nor heard, but assured himself was there anyway.

No light spilled forth as the door finally tapped into the brick wall. The darkness inside was so complete, it was as if no light from outside could penetrate the invisible barrier of the doorway. Somehow it was almost beautiful, mesmerizing. A darkness so complete it was like reality simply stopped at the edge of that tiny room. Consciously, Tony decided that the attendant would appreciate not having to walk out and lock the door himself. Subconsciously, something more, something vast and unrecognized, told him to step forward.

Step by step he approached. Intrigued, compelled, unafraid. Were his conscious decision the only thing driving him toward that restroom he may have closed the door and walked back to check the gas pump, which was nearly finished. It was, however, the weakest of Tony's motivations, and rather than closing it and walking away, he stepped into the small space.

As he crossed the threshold, into that infinite black, the room became illuminated, as though the sun had arisen in an instant and bathed the space in its golden light. He went from seeing the beauty of nothingness to seeing every disgusting detail of the room in a single moment. The graffiti carved into the walls near the lone toilet, the chips and stains in the porcelain seat and sink, the single, unlit light-bulb hanging from the ceiling, the moist bits of toilet paper wadded on the floor, the blackened grout between each tile of the walls, and, most curiously, the blue tarp draped over a humanoid shape curled in the center of the space.

Appalled and afraid, he stepped back quickly and hit an object that had to be the door. It could *only* be the door, and yet the room was clearly illuminated from outside, not from the lonely bulb that hung from the ceiling. He spun about, expecting to see a car's headlights and a person right behind him, but no. The sun had come up, and nothing, absolutely nothing blocked his way. A nothing so solid it could just as well have been a brick wall.

Just as the light did not penetrate into the exquisite darkness as he looked within, Tony was held from leaving. Trapped within the confines of the tiny gas station restroom with a lump that was probably the body of the last unfortunate soul to enter. He tried walking out several times, to hit his face on an invisible wall that felt much like stone. Tried turning on the light, which popped and broke. Tried pounding his fists on air that was becoming fetid and making him want to puke.

As Tony tried in vain to return to the outside world, a slight sound, like a plastic bag crinkling, roared in his ears. Only one thing in that room could make that particular sound, and his desire not to face it was nearly as great as his desire to leave.

He glanced back quickly, assuring himself that he must have stepped on the tarp, and, satisfied that the thing had not moved, returned to the doorway. Trying even harder to leave, he kicked at the nothing in the doorway, and realized that the floor had become slick as he nearly fell. At his feet pooled a thick red fluid. Already knowing where it would lead, his eyes followed the edge of the pool up to and underneath the unmoved tarp.

Shuddering, he debated removing that plastic sheet and confronting his roommate. On one hand, it was probably a deer or a coyote or something that someone was supposed to come pick up. On the other, it looked suspiciously human, and may have moved when he turned his back to it.

Tony maneuvered to what he thought was the head, careful to never take his eyes from the blue mass. As he knelt down, he noted that the blood was now seeping out from the tarp in every direction and, looking back to the doorway, seemed to be soaking its way up the unseen wall. A heavy beat reverberated in Tony's ears, but it was impossible to tell if it was his own heartbeat, or something else. He reached out and grabbed a wad of the tarp, careful not to touch the blood, and peeled it back.

Staring back from the floor lay Tony's own face. Ashen, decayed, but clearly his. The pallor made it seem that all the blood had drained away long ago. Shock made Tony stumble back and fall to his seat. Around him the red stain flowed up the wall in veins. The tiny restroom seemed to age around him as porcelain crumbled and paint peeled. Tony never saw the thing move, but a gurgling gasp escaped from the unmoving lips.

"You fall asleep, bud?" He heard the station attendant say. Tony opened his eyes with a slight start and looked over from his spot against the car. He didn't know how to respond. His eyes shifted to the bathroom door. Closed. Locked. It was night, and hard to tell, but definitely closed.

"Yeah, I guess I did." He finally said, and followed the man back inside to pay, wondering how he had fallen asleep so fast, when it usually took longer than he cared to track.

On the way back to his car Tony noticed that he had left dark, wet footprints on the concrete.

Teenage Sam Argues with his Mother about Heavy Metal

Samuel Lee

Ok. I know it looks bad. What with the pentagrams, inverted crosses, bones, skulls, demons, blood and/or gore. I don't really take this shit seriously.

This is just the way a soul might express itself when it feels choked by the banality of whatever purgatory it calls home. When home feels like an abyss, it is as if our bodies are attempting to purge themselves of all this oppressive ideology. This is especially true when a body is inhabited by a mind actively rejecting salvation.

Even more so in a body actively seeking damage.

I know it looks bad.

No I don't know why they felt it necessary to call the album *South of Heaven*, what the artistic motive was other than its fucking Slayer, and it sounded fucking cool and they probably knew we metalheads crave that kind of aesthetic, one in which the very act of listening feels like heresy. Like rebellion. Like freedom. Like hearing the death knell of another summer wasted in a driveway. Like I think you all owe me a graveyard.

This body craves damage so voraciously, and know this because I have quenched it countless nights in the pit where we crash into each other just to feel some connection.

I understand it all seems so abrasive you cannot fathom the joy that lies under the bedlam. The way the warmth of a Slayer album, a distorted guitar solo, and the thrashing blast of kick drums can sometimes feel like a mother's embrace when the night gets dark enough.

Which is perhaps why Alan has embraced it so much harder than any of us because when his mom went to prison on those meth charges and left him alone in that house he seemed ready to climb back into any womb that would take him.

I know. It looks bad, what with the black band t-shirts and black nail polish and no, I'm not ready to ask for help but I'm gonna be ok and this is going to help.

We are a few car wrecks away from that. See, I think I'm really smart right now but I'm fucking up in new and creative ways each day. I am crashing. This is just the soundtrack. This is just the way I process the anger.

We metalheads, we can never decide if we want to crash into each other or into ourselves.

We just want to feel the metal twist around us.

Each night we return bloodied to our basements, to dredge another Slayer album from a midnight that seems poised to never relinquish its darkness.

When we most need that warmth.

When our mothers feel too far away.

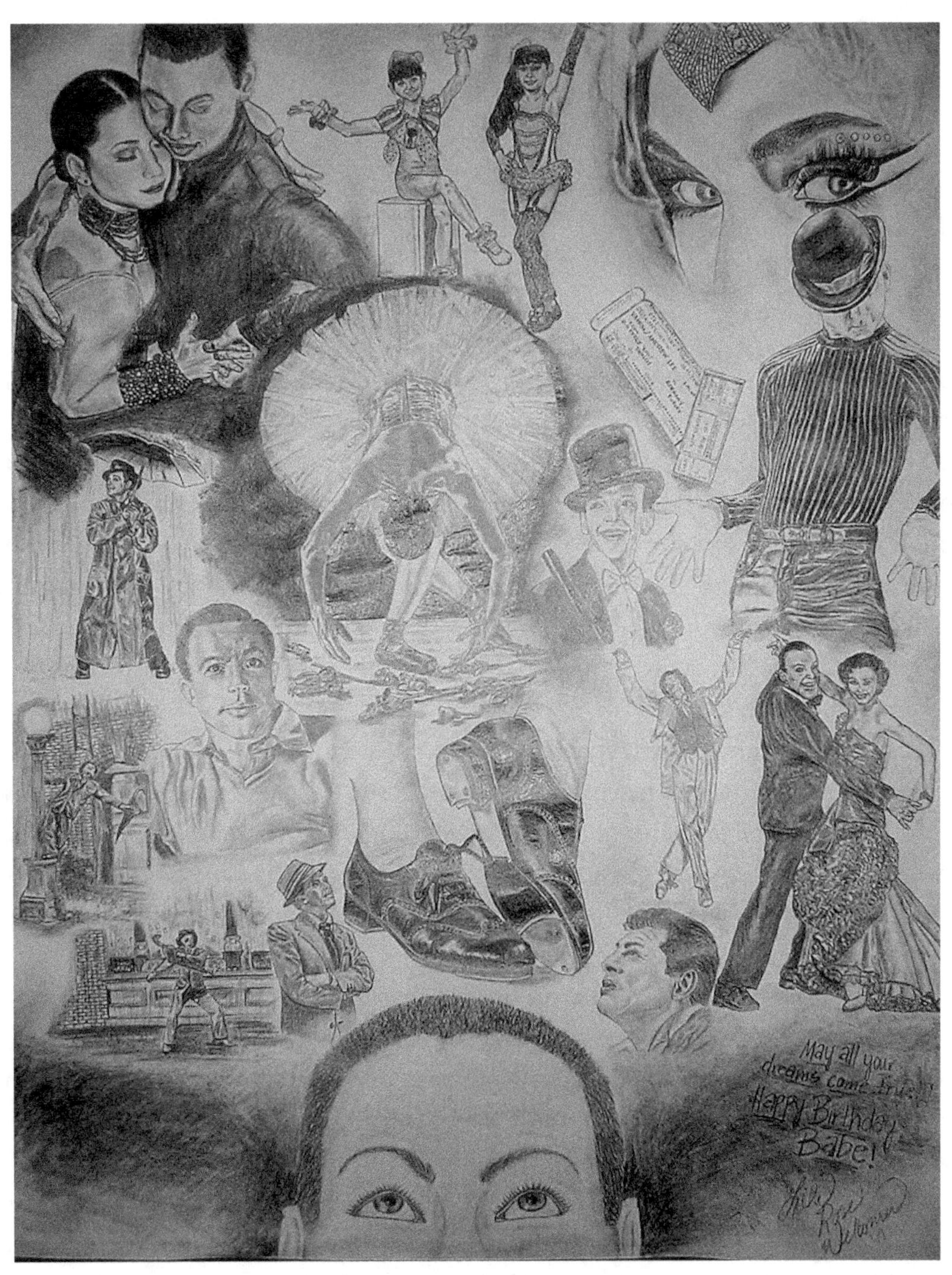

The Artist

Lila Rose

Toast to the Muse

Marilyn Loy Every

Oh, yes, She sometimes also told stories about this other woman in her head, her muse, that wanted to have her say. She would throw her head back, laughing, "There's my Sheila again." Sheila was that naughty girl—and, later the worldly woman, who wondered why She never smoked or slept around promiscuously as a young one, instead of being so damn demure. Or, why She didn't leave her young husband at the altar when barely eighteen, and drive that red convertible Chevy-of- a-wedding-car like hell to California where all the '60s "flower children" lived. Yes, Sheila was the one that made her say what was so, write raw poetry, tell crazy stories that really questioned her own logic.

Sheila was the one who whispered, "There is more than this!" I think it was Sheila who occasionally hissed in her ear, "Nothing is going to change. Let's just kick this to the curb and get the *flock* out of here!" Yet, She somehow managed to humor Sheila as well as listen to her good sense, trying to balance her life like any good Libra would try to do. And, She even gave Sheila voice by publishing some of what she had to say, just in case it made sense to any other woman.

She usually could shush Sheila up by relaxing her jaw and simply smiling with her eyes, with a sort of, "*Seriously?*" etched in code between her eyebrows. Sheila would roll her eyes as she watched her savor the happiness that her children gave her, respecting that She loved those kids like mad. And, Sheila softened realizing how She loved her grandchildren, too…with what She called "luscious love."

When She sighed contentedly, lollygagging in bed at night in the arms of her honey, Sheila would settle down again. Yet, there were times Sheila wondered what it would have been like if She and Sheila had packed up, taken off like friggin' homeless gypsies, with colorful skirts whipping in the wind, armpits with locks of soft, brown curly fur, and their vulvas smelling earthy—with no soap in sight. I must say, heaven forbid if they both would have become activists for justice at the *same* time!

Oh, yes, we all know that this woman climbed many ladders of accomplishment with a great deal of grit when there seemed to be "no way." *And, She did it anyway—her way!* I, for one, knew She really did love the inspiration gathered from the synergy of smart and honest people, and yet loved to retreat into the sanctuary of her own dimly candle-lit solitude, writing some sort of stuff She called "sacred poetry."

No matter what,… however,… Sheila could always count on resting her creative spirit on Marilyn's heart. Marilyn was Sheila's *Anam Cara*, that woman Sheila always called her "soul friend," that woman who barred nothing when She pitched her head back and laughed to the sky, that woman who really loved well—*really loved Sheila well.*

Seduction

Michael Skau

When she opened the door, I was stunned: she was wearing a black
lace shift so thin and transparent that practically
it had no value—but what a richness of vision
it held: the low-cut neck that looped the flesh
of her breasts, under lace her nipples black cherry;
and there like a kiss's home, shoulders and neck
bare and smooth; down below the hem a stretch
of luscious legs topped by buttock perfection.

"How do you like it?" she asked. "I bought it with you
in mind." Satyric fantasies in my head
whirled as I smiled my pleasure and gathered her
close in my arms. Stripping away my virtue,
I lifted the lace to stroke her back and said
with my tongue in my cheek that I'd like her in nothing better.

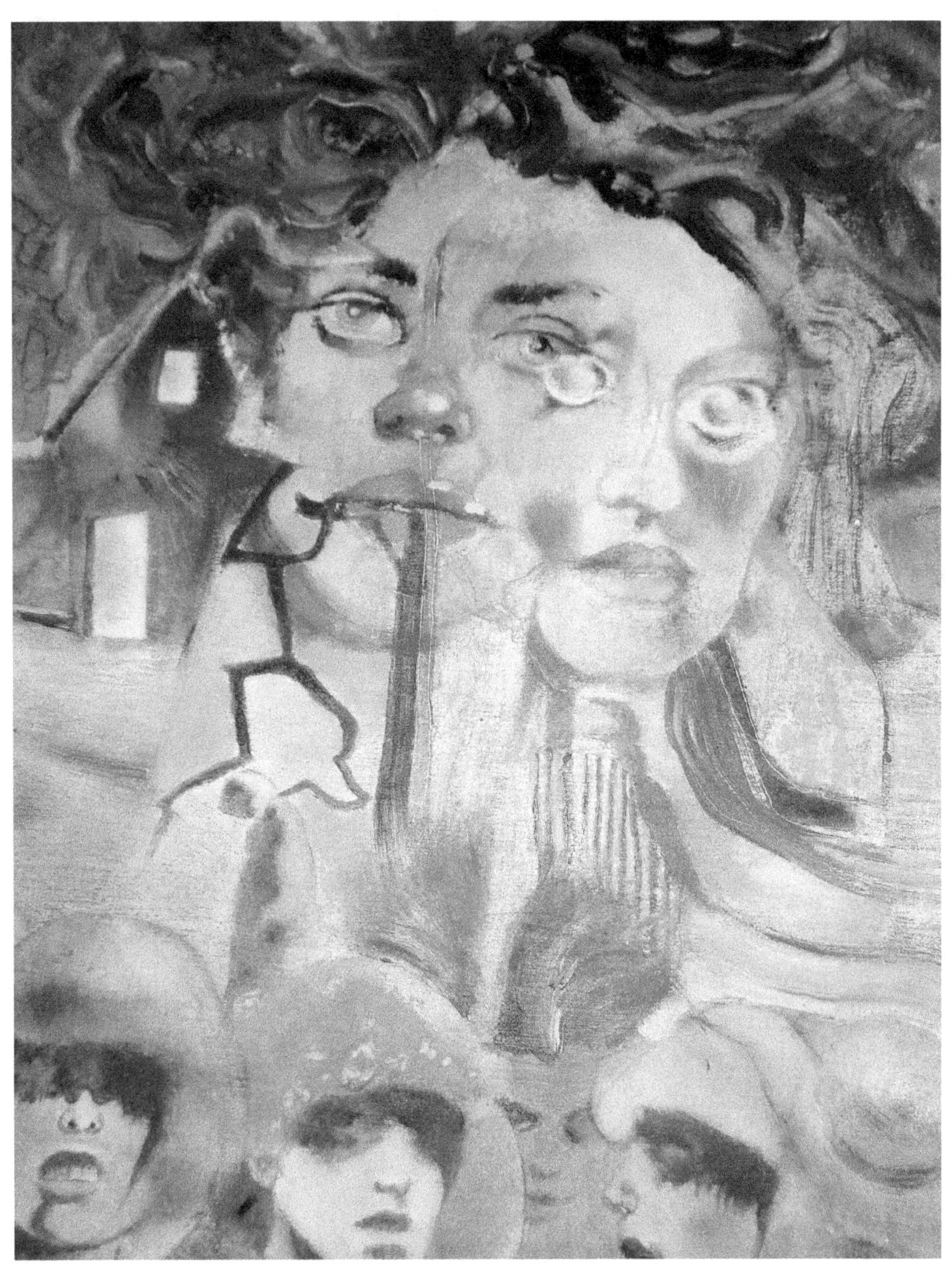

The Bride I

Rodger Gerberding

Still

Rick Kujath

Every time death stares someone down,
It sneaks up on someone else.
Your attention is drawn to what you know,
And death makes a fool of yourself.

A father, they say, has months to live,
They call his disease "terminal."
Two weeks later, the mother dies,
Without any warning at all.

Disease may take an agonizing time
For the Reaper to get his due.
But in that time you breathe, you live,
And by living, may meet him too.

Life is just a hidden-ball-trick,
A bait-and-switch if you will.
But death, the reaper, is very real,
Yet we live on, as we must, still.

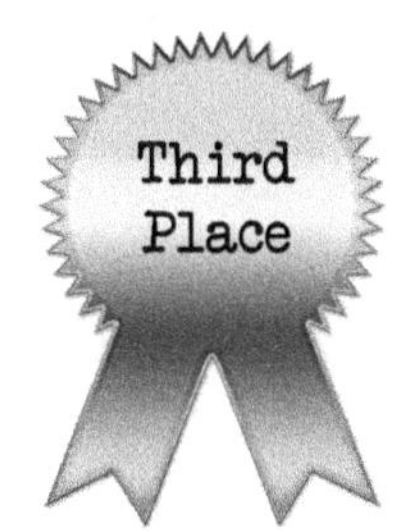

The Fish Tie, Mom, and Transference

Johnnye Gerhardt

Standing next to my mother's bed in the ICU, isolation shrouded me though family and close friends crowded the room. The click then hiss of a machine's diaphragm pushing air into her lungs echoed against the glass walls. My oldest daughter sniffled. My son's tennis shoe screeched against the linoleum floor as he shuffled his feet. A best friend and his wife leaned silently against a wall. My husband stood sentinel a few feet behind me.

A neurologist entered and stood on the other side of Mom's bed. My gaze left my mother's face and followed a silk, rainbow-trout tie leading to the physician's solemn expression. He introduced himself.

Gesturing toward the door, the doctor recommended that we step into the hall. Everyone but the doctor and I filed into the corridor. He pressed for my departure. Grabbing the rail on the side of the bed, I looked him in the eye.

"My mother and I have never kept anything from one another. What's the prognosis?"

Click. Hiss. Click. Hiss.

The man smoothed his tie. "Don't you think it would be—"

"Doctor. If my mother can comprehend what we're saying, not speaking in front of her would be the cruelest form of torture. Now, let's get to it. Is she brain dead?"

The physician cleared his throat then glanced at the door. His forehead glistened with perspiration. "The EEG is flat."

"So she is brain dead."

"Yes."

"If she woke up right now, what would she be like?"

"Just what you see here."

"Vegetative then."

"Yes."

Click. Hiss. Click. Hiss.

I could have sworn he bowed his head slightly as he backed away. But then I saw him only with my peripheral vision. My focus rested on my mother's unchanging face. I picked up her hand and stroked it. For the first time, she didn't squeeze my hand in response. Her hand rested unfeeling in mine. The crinkled, age-spotted skin looked tissue thin. Blue veins snaked from her wrist down to her fingers. I had never really noticed that before.

Everyone trickled back into the room. My mother's personal physician and a hospital nurse followed them. I lay my mother's hand at her waist.

"I want all support systems disconnected."

My best friend's wife gasped. My best friend broke into sobs. My daughter whimpered. My son left the room. My husband stood silent. My mother remained as she had been for the past 24 hours.

The doctor coughed. "Why don't you think about it? Make a decision in the morning."

I could see that he was distressed. The nurse glared at me as though I had passed a death sentence. A little late for that.

My voice lowered. "It is my mother's wish not to be sustained."

The doctor squirmed. The nurse crossed her arms and planted her feet. She was going to be a problem. I grabbed the railing. My knuckles turned white.

Click. Hiss. Click. Hiss.

"We discussed this many times." I gestured toward the machinery. "This is not what she wants."

The nurse and physician stood their ground. The doctor looked as though he was about to cry. He touched my mother's wrist in a way he probably had during the many years he treated her. His fingers lingered as though taking her pulse. He patted her hand as he released her. The urge to end my personal anguish faded. My grip on the bedrail relaxed.

"All right. But if she should start to fail, do not revive her."

***

The next morning, the same crowd gathered inside the room. Looking down at what used to be my mother, a thousand memories crowded the space between us. The delicate fingers that had braided my hair and caressed my hand now lay emptied of the love they so readily expressed. I rested my head on her chest in hopes of catching the rhythm that had comforted me as a fetus and reassured me as a child. But it was weak and difficult to hear. I touched her cheek.

Her personal physician and the cold-veined nurse entered. They approached the bed. I held my mother's hand and stroked her head.

"It's time."

The room went silent except for the click and hiss of the machine. The nurse stepped up to the bed. "What do you want me to do?"

My sorrow rose from depths I didn't know I had and I let it take over. I exploded with it. "Disconnect her!"

Everyone seemed to come to attention then as though they had caught my impetus. A doctor and nurse outside of the room stared through the glass. The isolation left me and I meant to fight for the woman who had fought for me all my life.

The doctor left, my son following him. Everyone else silently watched from a distance. The nurse stomped to the breathing apparatus and yanked the plugs from the wall sockets.

Click. Hiss. Cli. . . .

I lowered the railing and lay beside my mother as the nurse pulled tubes out of Mom's nose and mouth. I cradled her shoulders with my right arm and held her close with my left. The last, long exhale didn't come. She continued to breathe unassisted. I stayed beside her. The others hugged each other, wiped their eyes, and trickled out.

I agreed to a feeding tube for her the following morning. As the doctor put it, "It's one thing to let her die on her own. It's another to starve her to death."

***

My mother stayed in a coma for a month. Her body suffered the indignities of futility. The nurses at the hospice center turned her occasionally and emptied her colostomy bag when they thought of it or when we discovered it overflowing onto the floor. The hospice center called to ask if they could use her for a study of bedsores. I declined. "It's too soon," I said without anger, without feeling at all really.

Mom died while I was at work. My husband came to tell me at the department store where I was a counter manager. I rushed to the backroom where our coats and purses were kept. The young woman behind the counter smiled at me. It disappeared quickly. The urgency must have been visible.

"I need my purse."

"What does it look like?"

"Black, hobo, with brass fittings."

She pulled out a brown purse with a silver buckle.

"Black!"

The young woman grabbed a black purse. Not mine. I walked around the counter ready to knock her down if she tried to stop me. She grabbed another bag and held it up. Mine. I snatched it away from her without a word.

***

My best friend was with Mom. He said it went like she had told us it would. When I got there, I searched the ceiling for her soul. I believed in them then. When my daughter entered the room, I related the stories about death that my mother had told me.

I lifted my mother's hand and stroked her fingers. "Gramma said that when people die the tips of their fingers turn black."

We studied the darkening skin. "It's blood pooling in the extremities."

We talked about the mechanics of death and how natural my mother had made it for me. My daughter kissed her grandmother on the forehead. She took my hand.

"You want some time alone with her?"

I nodded.

I gazed down at the tiny, pale figure on the bed. "You're so cold, Mom. I don't think I've ever felt a cold like this."

It brought back memories from my seventh year when my father died. I touched his hand with my finger. It had been treated by a mortician so it was waxen and smelled funny.

"Remember when Dad died? I could barely see over the casket." The tears came. "I'm an orphan now."

On the way home, I cried quietly. I realized there was no one left to love me, not the way a mother does. There was no one left to marvel at my genius in everything or to tell me I was special.

Hating myself for wallowing, I checked my makeup in the visor mirror. An adult looked back at me.

"You're on your own, kid," I said to the woman staring back at me. Tears flowed down my face as a void opened in my heart.

My husband laid his hand on mine. "Are you all right?"

I leaned against his shoulder. "No. I need my mommy."

He kissed the top of my head and wrapped his arm around me. I didn't need my mother then. I needed him. Another kind of love cloaked my wounded spirit. I was going to be all right. I was going to tell her grandchildren what a marvelous, intelligent, honest, and brave woman she was. I looked forward to that.

The Janes

Kira Fish

It's a hot day out, though we are cold. The people down below, the courtroom audience, are sweaty and restless. The Janes and I stand together in the sealed-off balcony, the one whose floor collapsed years ago and was never replaced. There are nine Janes: myself and eight others. The other eight I call Blue-Eyed Jane, Green-Eyed Jane, Red-Haired Jane, Tall Jane, Heavyset Jane, Little Jane, Littler Jane, and Littlest Jane. We had other names, once. They're lost to us.

Each of us feels the pain of that loss. I remember the day it happened to me. I spent weeks on the road with a woman who was perhaps my mother or my aunt. We drove a station wagon across the country, fleeing from Oregon to Wyoming. ~~My mother my aunt~~ my female companion and I were running away from someone—~~my father my uncle~~ my sleepless nights. We ate gas station food and fast food and we always paid in cash. In eastern Wyoming, we abandoned the station wagon and bought a cheap Buick. After that, we headed into Nebraska. We didn't mean to stay here as long as we did. We ran out of money, and my companion had a way of earning more, quickly. I slept in the car while she did her business.

One night, I woke up to a brick sailing through the window above my head. Someone reached through the hole it left, disengaged the lock, and wrenched open the door. He grabbed me by the arms and pulled, hauling me out of the car, slamming me head-first onto the gravel of the otherwise empty parking lot. I don't remember what he said to me. Perhaps that would reveal too much about who I was and why my life had come to this. All I know is that shortly thereafter, I was in a lake. He didn't catch my companion, or else she would be with me, among the Janes.

We aren't in the Carvaterra County Courthouse in my honor, though. We're here for Heavyset Jane and Littlest, her daughter. We are here for each other, whatever the verdict may be. Heavyset Jane is short and thickset, with tan skin and brown hair and eyes. She is somewhere between 25 and 30 years old. Littlest Jane is a copy of her mother, but shorter, thinner, and about 3 years old. She rests across her mother's belly, her arms wrapped around Heavyset Jane's neck and her face buried in the trembling woman's shoulder. Heavyset Jane holds Littlest close as they listen to a medical examiner down below describe their injuries.

Fractures of the cranium, caused by several strikes delivered by a blunt instrument. Fractures around the eye-sockets and jaws, presumably from a steel-toed boot. *Shattered teeth. A mangled ear. Fractures of the cervical vertebrae, fractures of the clavicles.* Heavyset Jane doesn't show it, though. She retains whatever beauty she had before this happened to her, when she was whole and unbroken. Her eyes, though. Sometimes, when I turn my head to glance her way, I see bruises around her eye-sockets or crimson fluid welling along the tops of her cheekbones. Sometimes when she turns her head, her eyes are dulled with pain.

Littlest, though…Littlest Jane doesn't often leave her mother's side, but when she does, she shows what he did to her, shamelessly. She gazes at people with eyes full of tiny broken capillaries. She doesn't hide the chain of bruises around her neck. Today, though, she presses one ear into her mother's shoulder and covers the other with her hand as the man below her tells his audience about the clothes she was wearing, about the place where they found her and her mother.

The two of them ended up in a hilly badlands area at the extreme northwest edge of Carvaterra County, and were discovered one early spring morning by a rancher while he was examining his fences. Someone wrapped them in a beige tarp and left them in a dried-up creek bed where the lip of the ravine hid them from the view of motorists on the nearest county road. Earlier in the trial, the rancher testified that he first believed them to be a load of junk that had fallen out of someone's truck, but got queasy and decided to investigate when he noticed a matted lock of long, dark, hair sticking out from below the tarp.

Poor man. I know the ones he found haunt him to this day. Sometimes his thoughts drift up to where we sit and whisper his regrets to us. Perhaps if he had gone out sooner, he might have caught the one who did it, or have preserved more of the evidence. Perhaps their faces would still have been recognizable, and the police could have compared them with photographs of people who were missed. There were no matches with anyone's DNA, and as for dental records and facial reconstruction, Littlest Jane's reconstructed face went unrecognized, and she had never been to a dentist, and Heavyset Jane's teeth and jaws were crushed beyond the use of those methods.

That wouldn't work on me, no matter what condition they found me in. There were no Amber Alerts, no missing person's reports, no faces on milk cartons. The only person in the world who was looking for me, found me. He gave me my place with the Janes.

Blue-Eyed Jane and Red-Haired Jane sit together, whispering. They knew each other before, though they can't remember how—their best guess is that they ran away from home together and suffered the consequences of their newfound freedom. They are a little bit older than I am, maybe sixteen or seventeen. Red-Haired Jane has a deep cut on her neck. Blue-Eyed Jane has a similar one on her side. They don't bother hiding them. They were just passing through Nebraska when it happened to them, like I was. I don't know what they're talking about, though I could find out if I cared.

Come to think about it, that's how a lot of us ended up as Janes. We were just passing through. I imagine that this is a nice enough place to settle down, if you're the settling-down type. All the years I've spent here since, I've watched people passing by with their kids and their backpacks and their faux cowboy gear and seen a place meant for the strange and the forgotten—dusty purists and happy weirdoes. I think Tall Jane and Green-Eyed Jane were from around here, though, as well as Little and Littler. They look like it—clothes from bargain chain stores, Little Jane and her "big girl" cowgirl boots that her dad bought for her when she had to have her two front teeth pulled. Littler Jane's parents, whoever they were, never cured her of sucking her thumb, though I doubt that that's a Nebraska thing. I don't know much about who I used to be, but I know I'd have been embarrassed to still be sucking my thumb when I was somewhere between four and six years old.

Weird and misplaced as we are, we all bring our attention to the floor below us. Time passed while I was lost in thought—days, it seems. This trial has gone on for months, already. Now something in this room has shifted. They've reached a verdict.

The judge—I've forgotten his name already—waits expectantly for the jury. The Janes and I lean close to the edge of the balcony railing, to the point where we'd be in danger if we weren't already beyond that sort of thing. Heavyset Jane and Littlest Jane are still huddled together on a bench. We don't look at the man and his lawyer, sitting on the defendant's side. We don't give him the honor of acknowledging that he exists.

"Guilty?" Blue-Eyed Jane whispers.

“Didn’t hear,” says Red-Haired Jane.

“Will you two *listen*?” says Tall Jane. She’s much older than the rest of us, and seems to think herself to be our chaperone because of it.

Then we hear it. A voice from down below, ringing out through the room over the sound of fans running and people shifting in their seats, calls the words we’ve all hoped to hear.

He’s guilty.

We already knew he was guilty. Now everyone else knows, too.

He’s guilty of a thousand things, but right now, he’s guilty of harming the woman and girl whose names he refused to tell to the police, who weren’t known to be his wife or daughter yet for some reason were living on his property. He was caught by the tiny blue left shoe he failed to remove from his home, the one that was a perfect match for the shoe on the tiny right foot of a girl whom he’d harmed because she wouldn’t stop screaming. He forgot about the hairbrush full of Heavyset Jane’s hair, which had fallen behind a toilet in the tiny home they shared, and he did not know about the skin cells from his arm that were caught in the tarp as he did his best to hide them. He knows, now, and so do we.

The Janes are having a field day up in our floorless balcony. Blue-Eyed Jane makes a whooping noise and Little Jane jumps up and down, as if we’ve just found out that their favorite team won the Super Bowl. Red-Haired Jane grins and gives the judge a round of applause, though she knows that he can’t hear or see us. Only Tall Jane and I remain quiet. Tall Jane leans over and places a hand on Heavyset Jane’s unoccupied shoulder, prompting the rest of us to turn and see poor Heavyset Jane’s reaction.

Littlest and Heavyset Jane are trembling more than usual, their forms shaking with what may be relief or rage or pain. They don’t speak. Tall Jane reaches up and pats Heavyset Jane’s head, before backing away. Odd, that people like us would need to be given space, when we technically occupy none.

“Maybe we should leave them be?” I say.

Tall Jane nods. “We’ll be downstairs,” she murmurs in Heavyset Jane and Littlest’s direction.

Downstairs, we watch people file out of the courtroom. A few of them are crying. The guilty man’s family, perhaps? Some spectators who heard the list of Heavyset Jane’s injuries? That was days ago, though. Weeks, even, depending on how badly time has slipped away from me.

"I wonder why they're here," says Little Jane.

"I don't know," says Green-Eyed Jane. "Maybe they were bored."

"Maybe they watch too many crime shows," says Red-Haired Jane.

"Some of them are probably here for work," says Tall Jane. "Reporters and lawyers and whatnot."

Or maybe they actually cared about seeing some justice for Heavyset Jane and her daughter. I'm not going to snoop around in their thoughts, so it's not like I'll ever know.

Heavyset Jane and Littlest do eventually appear downstairs. By then, most of the people have left the building, and life at the courthouse seems to be returning to normal. Sentencing will happen another day. It's time for everyone but us to go home, eat dinner, and plan on what to do tomorrow if they hadn't done so already. The Janes and I remain. We stay with Heavyset Jane and Littlest.

"How do you feel, you two?" asks Red-Haired Jane.

"Tired," says Littlest. "Mommy, I want to go."

Heavyset Jane sighs. She's still holding Littlest close, like the little girl might disappear if she releases her.

"Soon, baby girl," she whispers, then to us, she says, "I'm not sure how to feel. I can't say I'm happy. If this were something to be happy about, I'd have a name and family again. Littlest would be starting pre-school and I'd be at work."

"I know," says Red-Haired Jane. "But it is what it is, isn't it? Aren't you at least a little bit relieved?"

"I suppose I am," says Heavyset Jane.

"What will you do now?" I ask.

"I was thinking about that," says Heavyset Jane. "Now that this is over, Littlest and I are going to go."

"Move on?" asks Green-Eyed Jane. "Can you?"

"Yes," says Heavyset Jane. "Something happened, earlier, during the announcement. I think we're finally free. I hear that happens, sometimes…"

"I've heard that, too." Tall Jane smiles, though it doesn't reach her eyes. "Well, see you around sometime."

"See ya," I say.

"I hope you end up somewhere nice," says Littler Jane.

The others say their goodbyes, too, and then Heavyset Jane and Littlest are gone.

"Must be nice," says Red-Haired Jane. She sighs a little, glancing around the room at the rest of us.

Maybe someday, that will be us, too. Someday, my female companion—my mother or my aunt—will finally come forward to claim me. Maybe they'll catch the man, the one who put me in the lake. Perhaps he never caught her, or perhaps someone else caught him. Then again, maybe someday water will run uphill and the sun will set in the east.

There's nothing else to be accomplished here tonight. We'll reconvene when necessary. Until then, the Janes and I part ways. I go back to the lake with the gravel parking lot, surrounded by bluffs and tall, dry grass. When I'm here, I like to take in the calmness of the water and scare the living daylights out of the occasional fisherman or swimmer. Tonight, though, the only people near the shores of my lake are a family with two children, a toddler boy and a girl who is perhaps seven years old, around Little Jane's age. The girl sees me and waves as I pass their fire, to the bewilderment of her mother and father. I wave back.

For perhaps the thousandth time, I step into the water of the lake, wishing I could dig my toes down into the wet dirt. Something is different tonight. When I stick my hand down into the muck, I pull something out—a metal bracelet that looks like it would fit my wrist.

Maybe someone dropped it, I think. But it has clearly been here for quite a while. The rust and the wear suggest that it has been here for years, and something tells me that it once belonged to me.

Why now? I ask myself. Why after all this time? Nothing answers me, of course; these types of things follow their own schedule. I turn the bracelet over. In faded silver letters it reads, *Courtney*. It's the perfect name for the no-longer Jane who stands in the moonlight.

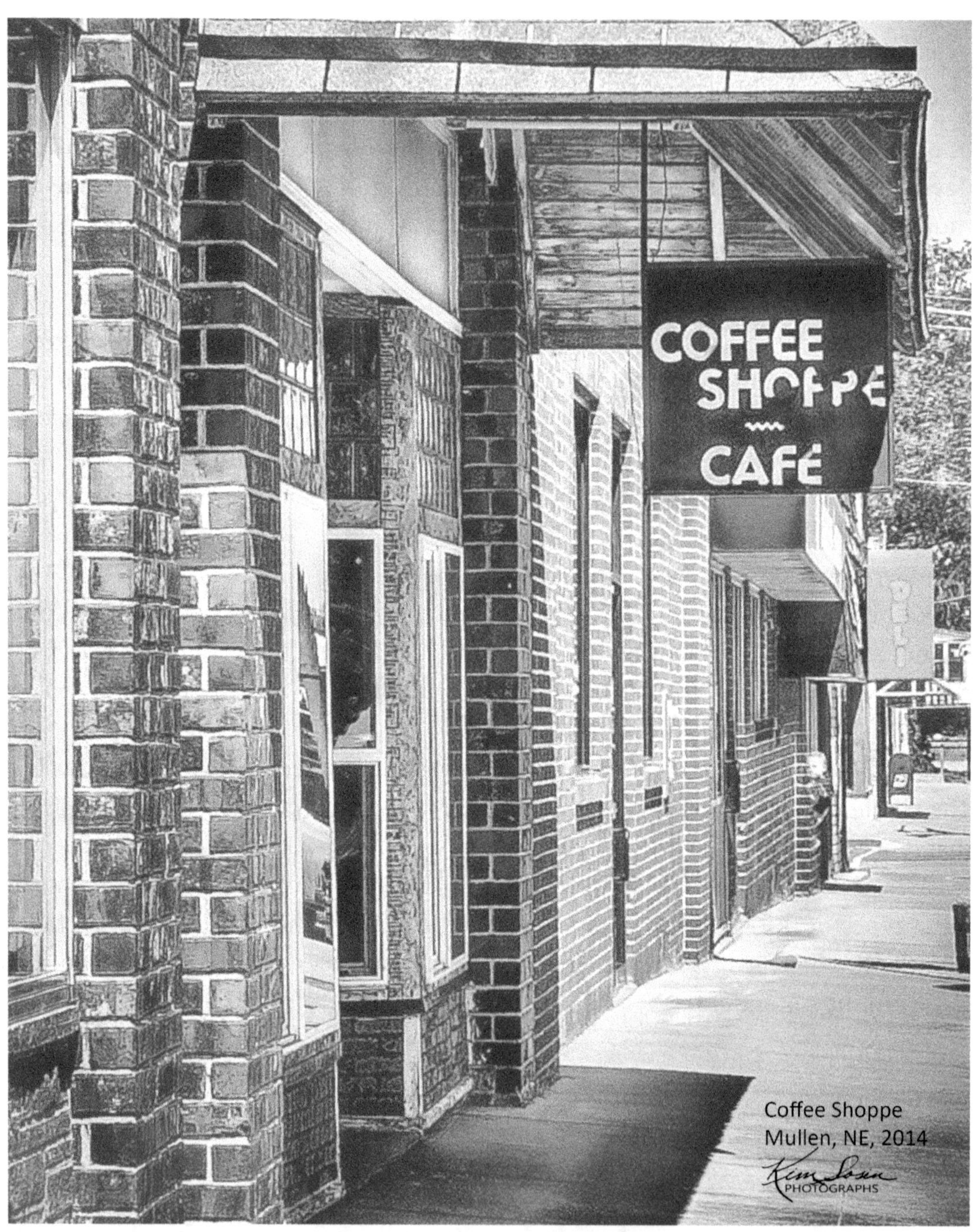

Coffee Shoppe

Kim McNealy Sosin

The Rural Rain Café
Morning Thoughts over Coffee

Kim McNealy Sosin

Morning, Alma, guys. Coffee smells good!
Whoa, Alma, sexy short skirt today!
Hey, Bob, pull up a chair.
You guys stop smirking!
Alma, more coffee and a sugar donut.
Dear god, I need a rest from these guys.
Bob's here now, the tips will roll in.
Right, he's as tight as the rest of you.
How about a warm-up all around?
I want to get this over with in one trip!
Morning, Mike, Jack, how's it going?
Random gods of weather
messing with us, always.
Not bad, we got 50 hunnerts last night.
Thank you rain god, at last!
Really, that much east of town?
Darn, why is my farm always left out?
We only got 10 hunnerts.
My usual bad luck; my everything
is that farm.
Mike, did it rain north of town?
Yeah, gauge read 70 hunnerts.
Lucky bastard!
Wow, that's wonderful!
Damn, why wasn't that on my farm?
Nah, I mean it could be, but
Listen, you guys, I still have
headaches out there.
I'm still planting, don't need the mud.
Friggin' rain gods never get this right.
Junior has to go back to
school tomorrow.
So he won't have to fight this farm for life.
I won't have any help.
Oh, I forgot your boy's in college.
I wish mine was smart enough
to get out of here.
So, how's your wife?
Word around town, she's dying.
She's not well at all, Doc can't
figure it out.
I've never been so scared!
Looks like we'll take her
to the Med Center.
What if they keep her, hook her up to
tubes, never comes home?
Ah, I'm really sorry to hear that.
Oh hell, I wish I hadn't mentioned that.
Sorry…
Do you think it will rain again tonight?
Whew, good save and just in time!
Nah, we're probably cooked for a while.
Cooked, wrung dry, always on that knife
edge.
Last year was dry, too.
Every damn year this land is dry except
for when it floods.
Yeah, except for that one weekend.
And damned if that downpour didn't
ruin my new planting.
There's Jim! Hey Jim, did you get rain
last night?

At Grandma's

Judy Lorenzen

I'd stay at her farmhouse
in Raymond, Nebraska,
and when evening skies
filled the kitchen window
with a cat or two,
Grandma would say,
"Time for bed."

We'd walk into her bedroom,
oblong mirror reflecting our faces,
mine watching hers.
Her white gossamer threads
swirled upon her head,
came down
bobby pin by bobby pin—
like snow falling on the fields,
ermine shawl on her shoulders—
she'd brush away the day's distress.

Sometimes I'd sleep by her,
smell her Chanel No. 5 perfume
all night,
sweet dreams—
her long shimmering hair,
on her pillow—
moon-spun rays shining on snow—

In the morning,
she'd rise to the rooster's crow,
snowy egret rising
to take flight,
carrying away the night.

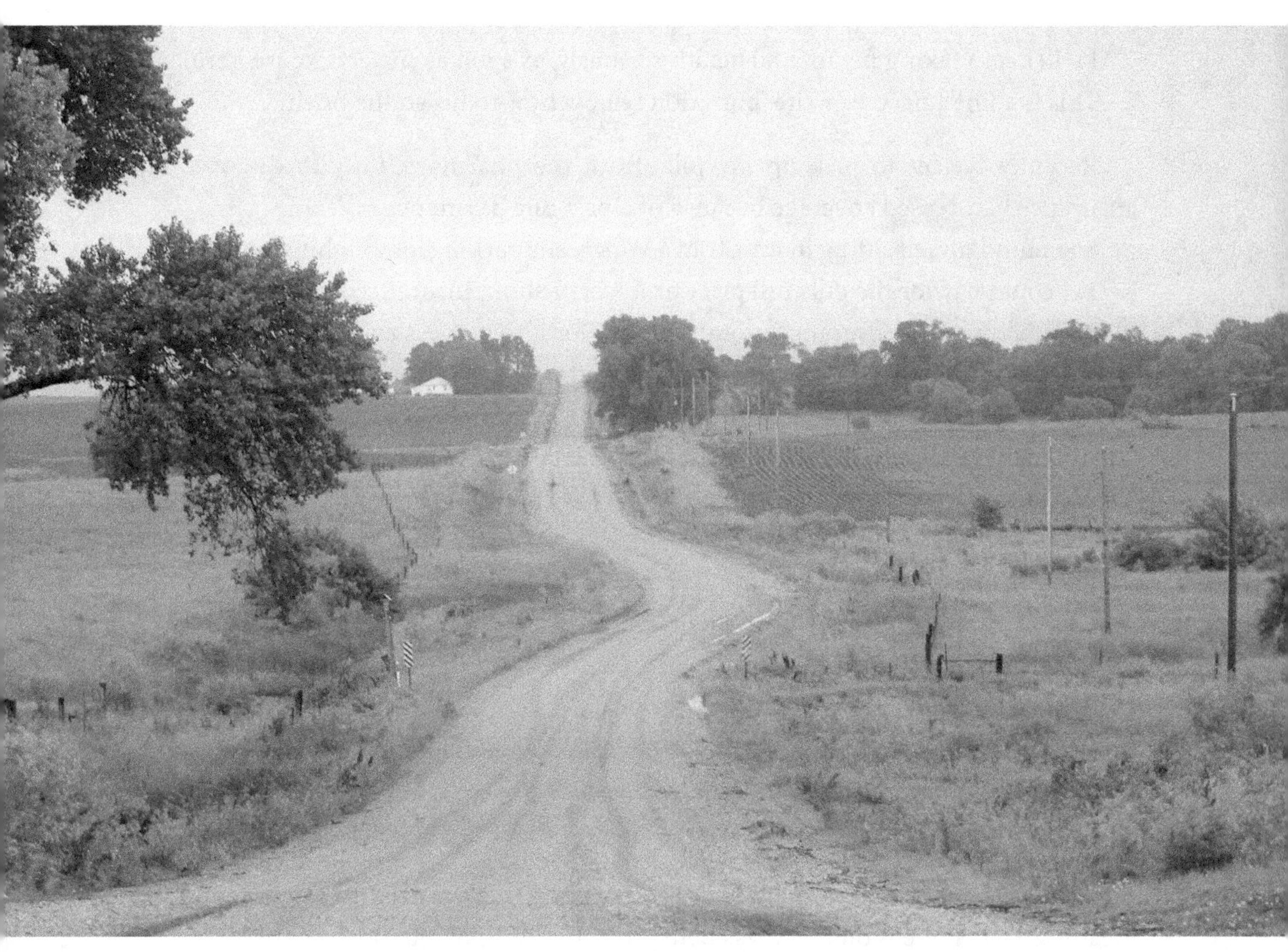

The Road Less Traveled

Chris Richter

At the Corner of Happy & Healthy

Samuel Lee

I will begin taking my mental health seriously, as soon as (insert excuse here).
This is a line I need to write, but I don't know how to finish the poem.

Recently I went to pick up my pills from the pharmacy, only to discover my insurance had ceased coverage because of a past due payment.
So I found myself sitting in my car in a Walgreens parking lot weighing my options:
1. I could pay for the pills full price and worry about insurance next paycheck,
2. I could pay the insurance premium, wait for it to process and then buy the pills, hoping I don't have a panic attack in the meantime
Suddenly, I consider a third option. One which has bounced back and forth since turning 26, purchasing this new insurance, and realizing how much it would really cost to keep me balanced
The third option is, obviously,
Just don't buy the pills. I mean,
You probably don't really need them. Dude.
You're probably just fine.
Depression and anxiety are all in your head.
Which is true, I mean, that's why they're called mental illnesses.
Honestly, I'm not sure how this all manifested.

Someone had to pick my head apart
Albeit briefly, to determine which illnesses had metastasized to my gray matter.
Reading each ailment off like I was being introduced to old family members.

I was 19, sitting across from
A court-appointed therapist,

Suggesting I get prescribed some drugs.
After getting busted with drugs.
Which is to say, I didn't have a great track record of saying no to drugs.
But suddenly I was being introduced
To new family members
Depression, meet citalopram
Anxiety, meet bupropian
I'll just let you all get acquainted.
Honestly none of this makes much sense.

Sometimes I try to get right.
Sometimes I just go left.
This is a line I need to write
But this is a poem I cannot finish.

I keep returning to the stories I was told
When I was young, of these people
Simply living with their mental illness
As if suppression of emotion
Was somehow a victory.
"See how strong they were?
How they never addressed
The trauma? They were taught
To ignore the internal
Dialogue pressing against their skulls
And they never allowed the dreams
In which they screamed
To affect them.
At all. Ever."

But see how they became consumed
Nonetheless. See how useless they became.
All dried out and full of dust.
Of no use to themselves or anyone else

At what point do we admit that admitting weakness is not itself weakness?
No, at what point do I admit
That I need these stupid pills.
Without them I am
Of no use to myself or anyone else.
And maybe that's the point.
It's not about me. It never was.
I want to be present. To stay afloat.
If I can do that,
Who knows?
Maybe I can finish the poem.

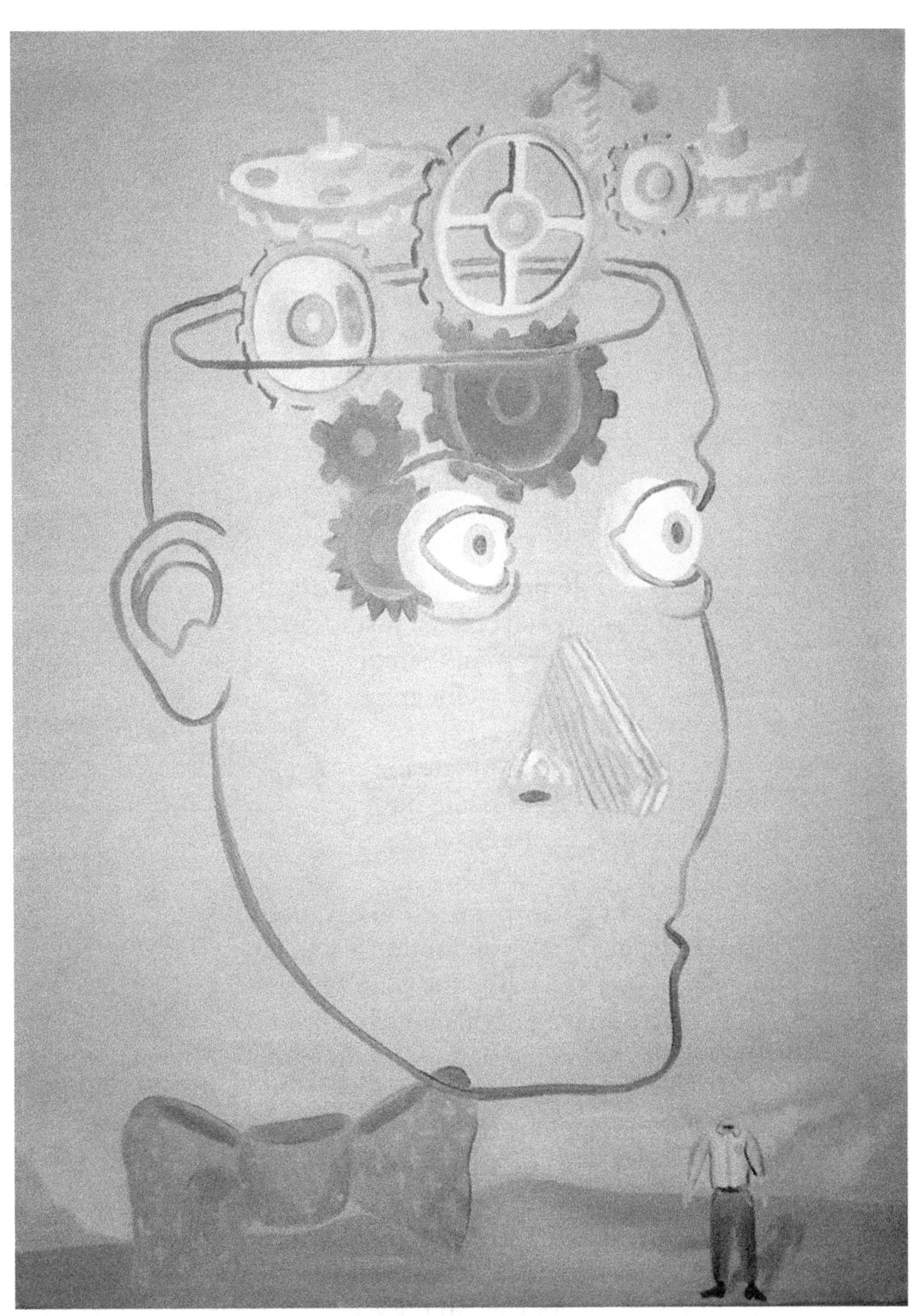

thinking

Joe Pankowski

I Do Not Use the N Word

Frank S. O'Neal

I do not use the N word
Will you simply see?

I do not use the N word
Do you know its History?

I do not use the N word
It is after all created just for me
Purely and Simply
To Defile me
Mortify me
Humiliate me
Ridicule me
Embroil me

And we use this word so cavalierly
Does that act make you footloose and fancy free
For as we still battle the chains of slavery
Why do we call this noun so proudly
When will the day come that we finally remove Masser's Revelry
I will end this tyranny
I will end this debauchery
I cannot be consumed by the elephant and their duality
I will end THIS vestige of slavery
I do not use the N word
Can you simply see?

I am NOT a MINORITY
I AM SOMEBODY

Once More with Feeling (Old)

Deirdre Evans

My skin is thinner,
rivered with wrinkles,
my hands, oh my hands,
I don't know the back
of my hands anymore.
I don't know anything
like the back of my hands
anymore.

Everything works okay,
good enough to get by,
and if the grey matter is now
more wrinkled, well,
that could be a good thing.
More room for memory,
my data coded, nestled
in my sheltered, convoluted
retrieval Rolodex
mixed metaphor of self-knowing.

I'm tired of absorbing new metaphors.
I will not carry a smartphone.
I will not update, I will not update,
I will not update.
I am ready to crash.
I will embrace the blue screen.
I will roll my skinny jeans
eat a low-carb diet
with an occasional piece of fruit.
It might be a peach.

Winter 70, Year 394

Daisy Lorraine Brandt

I awoke with a jolt and blurry vision thanks to the watery muck my eyes had excreted. A dried river of tears tattooed the left half of my face and a pond of saliva lay in the center of my sleek desk. I blinked several times to adjust my sight and scanned the luminescent classroom packed with thirty pale faces staring at me with eyes as wide as saucers. The empty walls blazed a glossy silver and the gibberish on the gigantic glowing holoscreen in the front of the class gave my head a slight twinge.

Then my gaze fell upon my undoing, my Instructor: Mr. Tholm. He was a half meter away from my desk, bending forward with his robust stomach nearly falling out of his tucked shirt. The hair he'd attempted to comb over his bald spots was dangling in front of his bifocals; his hairy hands were bunched up in fists against his hips. He was a glowing red demon against the radiance of the twinkling ceiling lights.

"Miss Knight. Please… explain to me why you assume that this type of behavior is acceptable in my class!?" His bitter voice boomed against the thick walls of plaster that made up the classroom. My spine grew rigid at the sound.

I couldn't find my voice for a few seconds, but when it finally came it was raspy and hurried.

"I-I just wanted to get some rest is all," I replied bravely, forcing myself upright. "I haven't been sleeping very well these past couple of days because of all the compartment-work you've been giving us, so I thought…."

"You thought what?! You thought you had the permission, the audacity to sleep in *my* class and then blame *me* for your irresponsibility?!"

Fires of cobalt blue smoldered in my Instructor's eyes. I shut my mouth.

He sighed, wrinkling his forehead with his hairy fingers. "Why must you always be such a pain?"

I said nothing and sat still, thankful that his anger had diminished, but unsure of how to respond.

"Well? Do you have anything to say, Miss Knight?" he asked.

I turned my head to the left, looking away from my Instructor and out the ceiling-to-floor window at the city below. Ivy's Hall of Discipline and Guidance is one of the tallest skytowers in the City of Aeris, so I had a stunning view of End's Ocean, which I took pleasure in gazing at, in that moment.

"Miss Knight!" Mr. Tholm shouted, his anger fully reclaimed.

"No!" I said, snapping back into reality.

"Excuse me?" my Instructor exclaimed.

"No, Mr. Tholm. I have nothing to say," I turned back to him, his thin lips curled.

"Oh, really? Nothing at all? Not even an apology?"

I realized my fault before he did.

"No, no. That's not what I meant. I—"

"I don't want to hear it, Miss Knight. I will speak with you once class has ended."

"Mr. Tholm, wait. I'm sor-"

"It's too late for apologies now, Miss Knight! You've already interrupted my morning announcements once, don't make the mistake of doing it again!"

I sighed with defeat as Mr. Tholm hobbled his way to the front of the silent room. I looked around to see every Student staring at me, viewing me with disgust, annoyance, or a mixture of both. Class had just begun, and my day was already off to a bad start.

It was about to get a whole lot more uncomfortable.

Once my out-of-breath Instructor reached the front of the class, he declared that he had a special announcement to share with us. And from the resentful look on his face, a rather foul piece of news.

"My apologies, Students, Discipline is just as necessary as Guidance is here at Ivy's Hall."

A couple of the boys in the front chuckled and took a sly peek back at me. I blinked in response. "Before *Miss Knight* decided to take a snooze, I was just about to share that there will be a new Student joining our class today, a rather… *unique* one."

I noted his emphasis on the word "unique" and the twitch of scorn at the phrase "new Student."

Mr. Tholm must hate this guy even more than he hates me.

I leaned forward, eager to see who was about to walk through the doors.

"Before I introduce him to the class, I ask you all treat him with respect. He has just as much right to be here as anyone else… for the time being. Now, please welcome your new classmate."

As Mr. Tholm hobbled to the sliding door of the classroom, I wondered what he meant by "for the time being" and why he wasn't acting as ecstatic as he normally does when a new Student joins the class. Slowly placing one foot in front of the other, our Instructor opened the door and gestured for the Student to enter. I stretched my head above everyone else's, eager to be the first to see who in Aeris this person could be.

Everything soon clicked into place as to why Mr. Tholm was acting so strangely. The new Student nervously stepped into the classroom, and everyone went silent. His skin was a rich orangey-brown against his grey, form-fitting outerwear. His hair fell in thick, dark curls that draped over his out-turned ears and square forehead. Light spots sported across his high cheeks and his chubby nose created craters that reminded me of the neighboring Hinterlands. His sad, deerlike eyes matched the darkness of his hair and suited his small, fragile frame. The kid wasn't much taller than me. But one thing was for certain: this boy was a Forgiven.

In the City of Aeris, our commanding charter, known as The Order, separates citizens into three distinct Classes. The Order deems certain Classes with more predominant attributes than others to keep the City of Aeris in a state of peace and control. I, alongside every Student attending Ivy's Hall of Discipline and Guidance, belong to the First Class named Prefection. Prefects are considered by The Order to be the superior citizens of Aeris. Our high status grants us with prestigious occupations throughout the city, including government positions within the Aerian Citadel.

This new Student was not a Prefect, however, but a Forgiven—an Aerian citizen belonging to the Second Class. As a step down from Prefection, Forgivens are common laborers and servants who receive mediocre education.

So why was this Forgiven enrolled as a Student in the highest-ranked Prefect academy?

Then, without being asked or told, the Forgiven boy spoke.

"Hello, um, Mr. Tholm's class. My name is Heron Lima, I am a Forgiven citizen living in the Median District of M-11. I am a new Student here at, uh, Ivy's Hall of Discipline and Guidance and I hope…"

The boy's soft, shaky voice was cut off by a fierce bark a few desks from me.

"Mr. Tholm, why is a Forgiven attending a Prefect-only academy?"

"Well, like I said before, he *now* has as much right to be here as anyone else," Mr. Tholm said, though his tone said otherwise.

"But Ivy's Hall is *Prefect-only*, plus he shouldn't even be allowed into the Inner Districts without Citadel permission."

A chorus of questions and comments flooded the air, and the Forgiven lowered his gaze to the floor.

"Yeah! If Forgivens aren't allowed within the Inner Districts, how did he get here?"

"My father is not going to be happy about me sharing a class with a Forgiven."

"He should at least be made to wear white. Our Class color is so much more sophisticated than that ugly grey."

"Do you think this has something to do with that new Article the Grand Assembly passed?"

I tuned the mindless jabber out as much as I could and focused in on the Forgiven boy. He was growing more uncomfortable by the second, and even though he belonged to a lower Class than me, I felt bad for him. I watched as his eyes began to tear up and his crossed hands tightened around his elbows. I know the feeling of embarrassment brought about by something you can't change. Heron didn't deserve any of this on his first day of Hall.

I stood up from my chair, cupped my hands around my mouth, and roared. "EXCUSE ME! HERON WAS TRYING TO SAY SOMETHING."

For the second time that morning, every Student turned to gawk at me, but this time I was being an interruption on purpose. I took my seat as I happily received a death glare from Mr. Tholm and a look of surprise from Heron.

"Go on," I motioned for the Forgiven to speak.

He stood silent for a moment and then continued.

"Um, thank you. I just wanted to say that I hope to make friendships with all of you and become a valued Student of Ivy's Hall."

"Not more valued than a Prefect!" shouted a boy in the middle of the class. Heron and I locked eyes as everyone else laughed, even Mr. Tholm let out a stifled giggle before he regained control of the class.

"Alright, alright! That is enough out of everyone," the Instructor said, still trying to kill his laughter. "Thank you, Mr. Lima, for your introduction and I hope you somehow evolve into that valued Student that you wish to become."

Pure sarcasm.

"Take a seat next to your friend, Miss Knight, in the back corner, near the window. I can tell you two will get along just fine."

I waved once and Heron nodded politely.

"Yes, sir."

"That's Instructor, to you," Mr. Tholm said.

More sarcasm.

"Uh, yes, Instructor, sir," Heron stuttered.

A few more giggles erupted from the front row as Heron made his way to the desk on my right and sat down. Mr. Tholm began his history lesson, which I skillfully blocked out to observe Heron.

I noticed that he had no Hall supplies. Absolutely nothing. No bag, no analog, no codexes, nothing. He simply sat and stared at the holoscreen Mr. Tholm was lecturing from, listening through a look of muffled fear on his face.

"Hey, Heron?" I whispered.

He shot me a look of surprise. I couldn't tell if it was because I was addressing him politely or because I was ignoring the Instructor's lesson.

"Y-yes?" he whispered back.

"Where are your Hall supplies?"

He looked down at the floor and shook his head.

"I don't have any."

"Oh."

The Forgiven Class isn't nearly as wealthy as the Prefect Class, so it made sense that Heron didn't have any Hall supplies. He simply couldn't afford them.

"I can type notes for you, if you'd like."

Heron looked confused. Why would a Prefect ever help a Forgiven when Forgivens were born to obey the First Class? Especially a Prefect belonging to such a heinous class of other Prefects? I didn't know the answer to either of these questions—all I knew was that I wanted to help him.

"Really?"

"Of course!" I whispered a little too loudly.

Mr. Tholm tossed us a look of suspicion, then turned back to his lesson.

"But, why?" Heron asked.

I shrugged my shoulders and reached into my shoulder bag, searching for a blank codex. My fingers felt the smooth, cool surface of the device without even looking. I powered my analog on and plugged my codex into the typeboard with a thin white cord. A few seconds later, the holoscreen loaded up. Heron's large eyes grew larger as he watched me in action.

"Do you know what any of this stuff is?"

To *my* surprise, he snickered quietly.

"Of course, I do. That codex is used to store the information transferred from the analog-typeboard. Why do you ask?"

"Uh, I didn't know you'd know about this stuff because… "

"Because I'm a Forgiven?" Thorns. He smiled with thorns as teeth.

"I'm sorry," I said, "I didn't mean to make you feel bad."

"It's fine," he said, shrugging, "I am just shocked to see that every Student here has one. The Hall I used to go to restricted analog use to the Instructors."

"Oh," I said, forgetting to whisper, "Let me start on these notes for you then—"

Suddenly a roar exploded loud enough to crack the windows of the classroom.

"MISS KNIGHT! ONE MORE INTERRUPTION OUT OF YOU AND I WILL REMOVE YOU FROM MY CLASS ROSTER."

I couldn't mess up again. I pushed my chair out from under me as I stood up straight, causing it to crash against the white tiled floor.

"My deepest apologies, Instructor, I was only trying to become acquainted with our new Student, sir!"

"Well become acquainted with that boy during the meal break!"

"Yes, Instructor, my apologies."

He streamed curses as I picked up my chair from the reflective ground. My face was flaming red as I took my seat and steadied my breathing as much as I could, slowly calming my nerves.

After a minute of recovery, I glanced at Heron. He sat stock-still, a bead of sweat draining onto his left cheek, with his gaze straight forward, unflinching. He didn't even blink. I huffed, but decided to type the notes for him anyway, even if he didn't want to talk.

The floating blue holoscreen had been booted up for a while now. A thin white line appeared, disappeared, and then reappeared every so often, signaling me to begin typing. I peeked over at Heron one last time and felt the corners of my mouth turn upward slightly.

I hope I can make a friend again. One I can keep. One that doesn't leave me.

I tuned my ears back to Mr. Tholm's lesson as my fingertips flexed against the cool typeboard. And before I began a summary of the Variant Rebellion, I headed the notes with my name: *Esma Knight.*

When my girls were little

Linda Robinson

When my girls were little
Seems hair was never brushed
Like flowing tumbling flowers
Silk ribbons blown and rushed
When my girls were little
Their hair swept off, aside
In bouncing fluffed disorder
Revealing smiles wide
Simple play and wonder
Compelling, strong, yet messed
I'd gaze upon their faces
And feel my heart so blessed
Those days spent growing, playing
Running, cheeks a'flushed
The breeze, the sun, the moment
Cared not, their hair was brushed

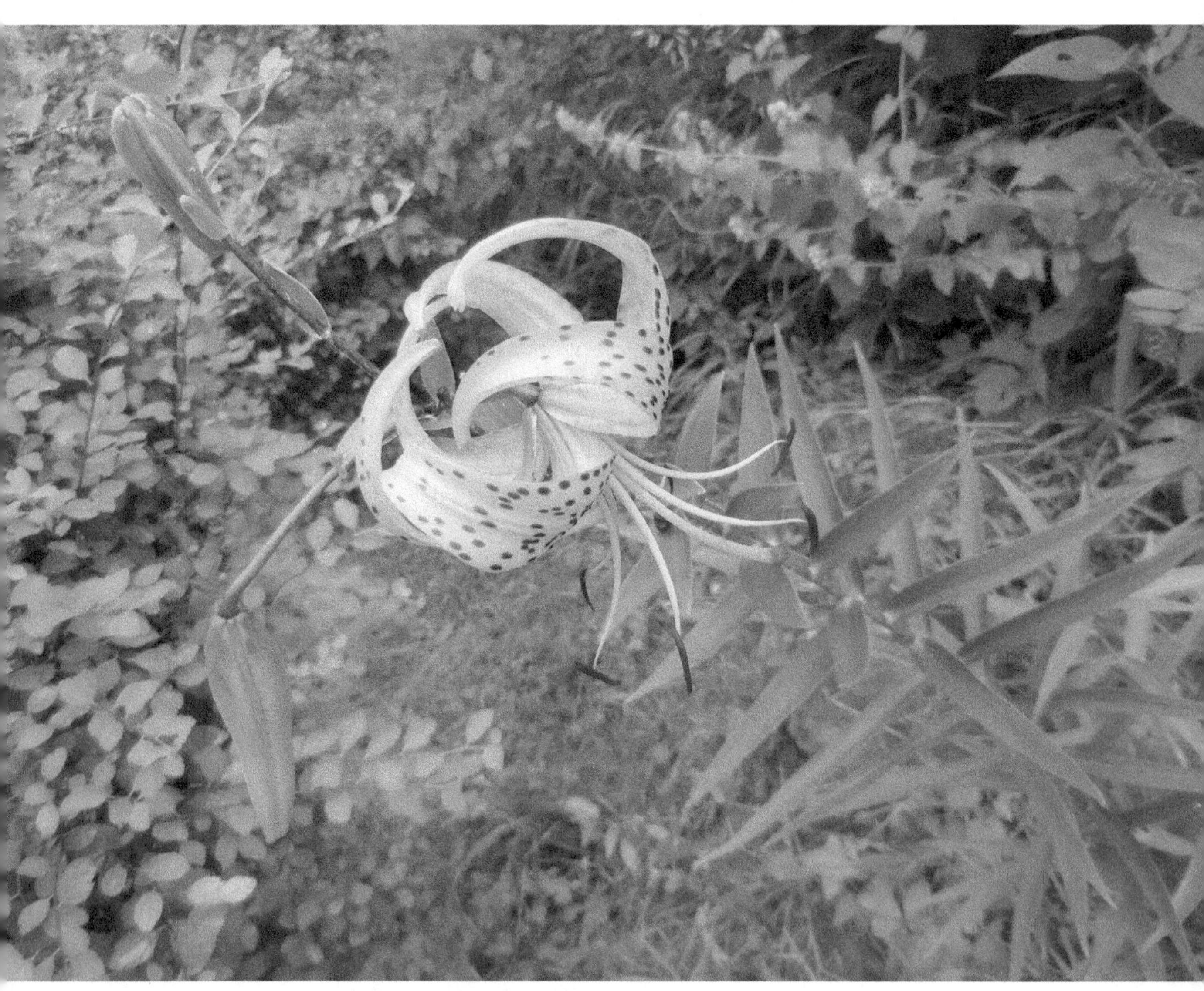

Tiger Lily

Robert Ericson

Loudest Silence

Gracie Ellis

You know what?
Stop saying I wish she told us
Because she did tell you
She was practically screaming it
She didn't use words, but she used actions

When she came out of the shower with red eyes
When she cried over the smallest things
When she came downstairs with dry tears on her checks
When she locked herself in her room
And never wanted to come out

She told you when she got angry over nothing
When she barely talked to you
When she started becoming uninterested in the things she used to love
When she started acting different
And started acting out

She told you when she never wanted to do anything anymore
When she stopped eating as much
When she started becoming "sick" more often
When she stopped hanging out with her friends
When she couldn't put what she wanted to say into words

So don't say she didn't tell you
Because she did
She was practically screaming it
How could you not hear her?
Now, it's too late…

Self Portraits as Crystal Quartz

Kellie Hayden

Our codes form,
stack for birth,
carbon, oxygen, or sulfide. Silicon
can hurt the most, because it's so
common, because so many of us have some
goddamn sob-story, some gunny-
sack full of kittens and stones
in a childhood river.

Our structures repeat. What we
are made of remembers each
biological fracture—we give each other
these serrations, terminating
into tetrahedral tines,
and we allow them because we'd die to hear
that we have our mother's nose.
We tend these bags of
mewling stones,
friction their paws warm,
because our aunt would have wanted us
to at least just *try*, to remember
our water-logged dawn.

Our aunt, who could never have
her own bed, who could never handle
the mountains when the seas
of little bluestem ached
within her green prism, who left
mounds of white foam
papers below her levitating soles
as the cats went quiet.
Polymorphic us, I and I and I
we shrink to wonder how far-reaching
these familiar ghosts are, and when
they will germinate into the void
after us.

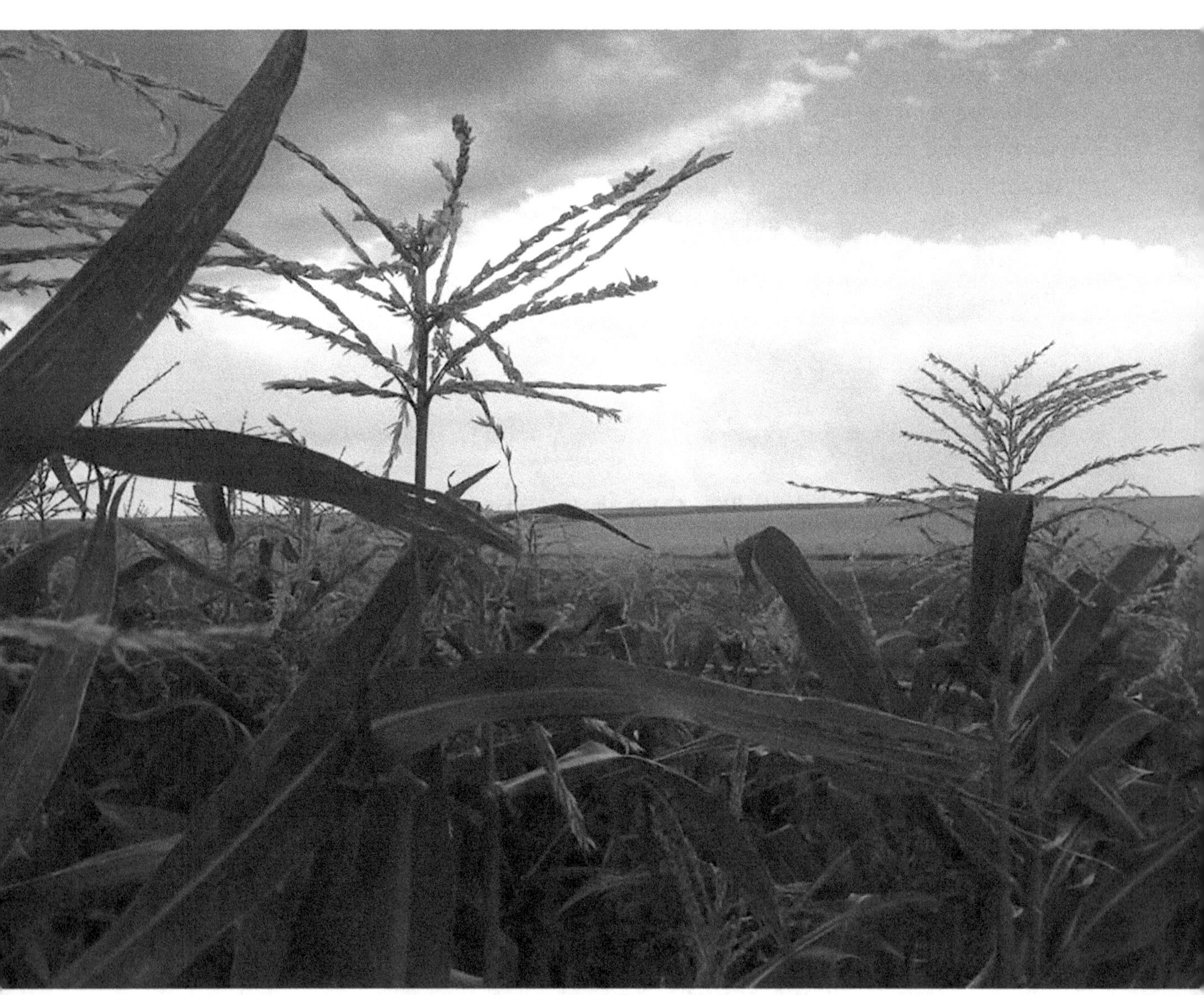

Weathered Corn

Donna Schluckebier

Conversations in a Cornfield

Johnnye Gerhardt

Papa clasped his hands on the edge of the table, bowed his head, and said grace. If Mama had been alive, he would have scrubbed the dirt from under his fingernails and left his seed-corn hat on the hook by the door. But she wasn't, and I guessed my cooking didn't warrant the respect.

From under my brow, I peeked at my brother, Buck. The tattered lace curtain barely covering the open window behind him billowed slightly. A fly trying to get past it ended up landing dead center on a flower pattern. Mama's favorite hen, Margarite, clucked just outside. Her two sisters joined in. I knew Henry, our rooster, wasn't far away.

Though it was hot enough outside to cook the chickens as they stood in the shade, the air in the one-room cabin pressed against my skin with a chill. A deep cut surrounded by a purple bruise marred one of my father's knuckles. It was the same color as the gash in Buck's lip.

"Amen," Papa declared and picked up his knife in one hand and his fork in the other. He held them as though he intended to do battle with what was left of Fancy Nancy, our last pig. A portion of her ribcage lay on the platter set in the middle of the table. It had been a bad year, so if there was such a thing as a skinny pig, Fancy Nancy was it.

When Buck opened his mouth to say, "Amen," I saw that two of his protruding front teeth weren't protruding anymore. They pointed toward the back of his mouth. I wondered if we would have to change his nickname but I couldn't think to what. His teeth were the only outstanding things about him.

"Ameth," Buck said.

"Amen," I whispered. Emma, my little sister, stared at the meat. I lifted the bowl of boiled potatoes and extended it toward my father. Papa stabbed the ribs with his fork and divided them in half. "Can't you see my hands is full?"

Papa hefted the meatiest and largest ribs onto his plate. He glared at me and slammed the butt ends of his knife and fork onto the table. He commenced to tearing off a rib and stuck it as far into his mouth as it would go. When he pulled it out, it was stripped so clean the fly wouldn't want it. Papa's cheeks bulged and grease trickled down his chin.

"I'm sorry." I set the bowl back on the table.

Papa took to glaring at me again.

"Well?" Bits of meat flew from his mouth when he spoke.

I scooted the potatoes toward him. He growled at me, so I scooped two of the largest ones onto his plate. Papa stabbed three more in the same manner he had served up the pork. That left just two, small, half-rotten potatoes and the nearly meatless, smaller ribs for Buck, Emma, and me.

Emma, who was only four and always hungry, would have to do without. Papa beat us if we shared. He had declared just Sunday last that when there wasn't enough to go around, Emma would go without. She was, after all, completely useless around the farm. She couldn't even gather eggs properly, having broken all but three in her entire egg-gathering career. I once told Papa that maybe if he stopped yelling at her, she'd quit dropping them. He slapped me hard. Emma broke all the eggs that day.

Papa pushed the potato bowl toward Buck a little too hard. It rocked, the table twisted a bit, and one of the potatoes fell out. It rolled toward Emma who eyed it and then my father. He urged it toward her with a finger. Emma reached for it but quickly pulled her hand back. The man was quick with a knife and nearly got her once.

The potato rolled off the table and splattered on the floor. My father stood. Since Buck shared the bench with him, he had to stand too or it would tip. Papa wasn't very handy at building furniture. We couldn't sit across from each other because the table wasn't wide enough. But it sure was long. And wobbly like the bench. When Mama died, I got her chair, the one with the cushion. Emma got mine, which was next to Mama's.

Papa walked around the table to where the potato lay. Emma's eyes filled with tears as her hands slid under the table. I knew she had them folded in her lap and was praying silently.

I stared at my plate but kept the corner of my eye on Emma. In my mind, I called upon God to strike down this man before he could hurt Emma who hadn't done anything.

When I was alone in the field, sometimes I screamed at God for taking Mama instead. It was Papa's fault that Emma was so jumpy. It was Papa's fault that the table wobbled. And it was Papa's fault that Mama died, and it would be his fault if Emma died too. I had hoped that he had worn out his demons on Buck but it didn't look like it. I thought God must have gone deaf.

With the speed of a feral cat after a rat, my father yanked Emma off her chair and shoved her onto the floor. He put his knee in her back to hold her there.

"You know we can't allow no waste. Emma here ain't had nothing to eat today 'cause she don't earn it. Letting that potato fall to the floor cost her a piece of meat. But me being in a generous mood, I'm going to let her have that potato if she wants it but she's got to eat it where it lies." He looked up at me and grinned. "Ain't no sense in you wasting your time washing a plate when you don't have to."

Halfway to standing Papa pushed Emma's face into the still steaming potato. She screamed in a sweet, small, frightened voice and then broke into tears. Without thinking I stood and walked toward her. Buck grabbed for me and missed. I rolled Emma over and scooped her into my arms. Steam rose from her scarlet cheeks and nose. Her whole body trembled. With an index finger, I pushed potato from her face. She sobbed. Papa walked back to his place at the table. Buck worked with him to pull the bench closer.

Papa sat down with a thud. "And what do you think you're doing, missy?"

Tears gathered in my eyes. "Emma's hurt."

"She ain't going to die. Get up to the table and pass me the butter."

For the first time in my sixteen years, I disobeyed. I eased more potato from Emma's face. I stared at the three freckles like a dotted line on her nose.

There's no telling what would have happened if I'd looked at Papa. I think that's what saved me. And I think it was that moment that taught me how to win. I focused on another part of her face so I could see Papa from the corner of my eye. He reached across the table and grabbed the plate of butter. It was as if he'd backed down in some way.

Over the years, there were more victories, each larger than the last until he finally, blessedly died. I walked into the middle of the cornfield that day and asked God why it took Him so long. He didn't answer.

What I Will Take When I Leave—Platte River Lament

Terry Lee Schifferns

I.
The first time I floated
in your gentle embrace,
in the blind of brightness,
minnows nibbling
at the sacrament
of tender flesh.

II.
The dip and glide
of three eagles
above the frozen river bank,
such passionate deluge
trapped beneath silent ice pack.

III.
The last chore of the night—
curled in the scent of wood smoke,
under Orion's watchful eye,
the ritual chill of bared flesh
christening fresh snow
star blessed.

IV.
The migration of cranes,
the manifest of lusty coos;
cracking the dawn,
the prophets of Spring
bound in an oracle dance.

V.
The Platte's smallest tributary,
shallow, but sure—
swimming through my veins—
inlet to my heart.

Writer and Artist Bios

Julian Adair

Julian Adair is a noted choreographer, dance educator, performer, arts photographer, director, author and native Nebraskan. She is a two-time recipient of the Theater Arts Guild Outstanding Achievement in Choreography Award and the 2016 winner for Outstanding Choreography by the Omaha Entertainment and Arts. Her photography records moments of choreography, using natural light, architecture, natural surroundings, and can be seen in her recent book *Advice to a Dancer: Wisdom from the Studio and Stage.* She is also publishing *Delightful Secrets of the Nutcracker*, based on her production of *Nutcracker Delights*, now in its 11th season. She is happily married to Steve Adair and together they have two daughters, Camille and Colette, both accomplished performers.

Lucy Adkins

Lucy Adkins grew up in rural Nebraska, attended country schools, the University of Nebraska, and received her degree from Auburn University in Alabama. She earned her MFA from the University of Nebraska—Omaha. Her poetry has appeared in many journals which include *Midwest Quarterly, Red Wheelbarrow, Rhino, South Dakota Review, Concho River Review*, and the anthologies *Woven on the Wind, Nebraska Presence, Crazy Woman Creek,* and the *Poets Against the War* anthology. Pudding House Press published her chapbook, *One Life Shining: Addie Finch, Farmwife*, and she has co-authored a book of non-fiction, *Writing in Community,* which won an Independent Publishers Book Award.

Daisy Lorraine Brandt

Daisy Lorraine Brandt is a sophomore at the University of Nebraska—Omaha, majoring in Creative Writing with a Concentration in Fiction. She has lived in Omaha, Nebraska, all her life, and doesn't plan on moving away anytime soon. As a trans woman and intersectional feminist, Daisy is heavily involved in social justice work to free marginalized groups from institutional oppression. Her writing emulates her passion for liberation, freedom, and civil rights. Daisy hopes her work becomes well-recognized one day, so she can create a change in the hearts and minds of her readers that can only be made through literature.

Marilyn June Coffey

Marilyn June Coffey, born July 22, 1937, in Alma, Nebraska, graduated second in her class of eighteen from Alma High School. She won a short story contest and a state oratory prize in her freshman year in college. The University of Nebraska named her Outstanding Senior Woman Journalist and published her research paper when she graduated in 1959. After living 30 years in New York and shorter times in Massachusetts, Nebraska, Kansas, and North Carolina, Coffey returned to Nebraska in 2004. Eighty of her poems have been published, one winning a Pushcart Prize, hundreds of prose pieces, and ten books. Three books—including *That Punk Jimmy Hoffa!*—are set in Nebraska.

Kaye de la Hulle

Kaye de la Hulle primarily writes poetry and short stories and occasionally has been published over the years. She sometimes publishes her work under her given name, Kay Strong. She has been a member of the Nebraska Writers Guild since 1993. In 1995-97 she authored a Single Parent Newsletter with world-wide publication for the Omaha Catholic Archdiocese. Currently she is writing her mother's life story. She is a life-long Nebraskan, having grown up on a farm in southeast Nebraska. *Daffodils* previously was published in the 2015 summer edition of the *Lincoln Underground Literary Journal.*

Sally Deskins

Sally Deskins is an artist, writer, and curator focusing on women and feminist issues in art. A 2003 University of Nebraska—Lincoln graduate in studio art, she worked in several Omaha arts organizations while developing her own work exploring motherhood, womanhood and the body, heavily inspired by her mentor and friend, late contemporary artist Wanda Ewing. She moved to Morgantown, West Virginia, in 2014 where she obtained an MA in art history and continues to write, curate, exhibit, edit the journal *Les Femmes Folles: women in art*, while serving as Exhibits Coordinator for West Virginia University Libraries.

Marilyn Dorf

Marilyn Dorf grew up near Albion, Nebraska, on the farm her great-grandparents homesteaded. As an only child, she spent much time reading and exploring nature. Her poetry and other writing has appeared in various publications, including *South Dakota Review, Coal City Review, Willow Review, Plainsongs, Northeast, Platte Valley Review, The Christian Science Monitor,* and *Nebraska Life,* the anthologies *Times of Sorrow/Times of Grace, Crazy Woman Creek, Nebraska Presence,* and *The Untidy Season*. Her chapbook, *This Red Hill,* was published by Juniper Press in 2003. She lives in Lincoln, Nebraska, with her dog, computer, and a houseful of books.

Gracie Ellis

Gracie Ellis is a high school student living in Grand Island, Nebraska. Some of her favorite things are writing, drawing, and photography. She has previously had one poem published. Gracie would love to be a journalist when she is older so that she can inform, entertain, warn, and inspire people with what she writes. In her free time, she enjoys playing outside with her brother, hanging out with friends, babysitting, and doing various watersports with her dad.

Robert Klein Engler

Robert Klein Engler lives in happy exile in Omaha, Nebraska, and sometimes New Orleans. He is a writer and artist. Robert holds degrees from the University of Illinois at Urbana and the University of Chicago Divinity School. He has received Illinois Arts Council awards for his poetry. Just google his name to find his writing on the Internet. Michael Morgan, writing in the *Comstock Review,* says that Robert Klein Engler "…is a poet of the first rank," whereas Andrew Huff writes in *Gaper's Block* that Engler's writing is "a sublime banquet of bullshit."

Robert Ericson

Omaha, Nebraska, resident since 1975. Born in DuBois, Pennsylvania, in December, 1941. BA in Applied Art, 1963, Penn State University. Retired USAFR colonel. Has two pieces in the Air Force Art Collection. Retired freelance artist and instructor of illustration, layout, typography, and advertising design. Designed, illustrated, set type by hand for, and letterpress printed, his own chap book, *Things I Never Noticed Before.* Skier. Pickleball player. President of Top Flight Badminton Club. 29 consecutive years as Cornhusker State Games Badminton Sport Director. With wife, raises Columbia sheep. Two granddaughters.

Maritza N. Estrada

Maritza N. Estrada is a Creative Writing major with a Poetry concentration at the University of Nebraska—Omaha's Writer's Workshop. Her senior thesis application in poetry has been recently accepted, and she plans to focus on including Spanish and English languages; literal and figurative residencies that explore the Pacific Northwest, Midwest, and Southwest; and borders of identity in relation to ethnicity and nationality. Her work has been published in the *Omaha World-Herald, 13th Floor Magazine,* and *The Flat Waters Stirs: An Anthology of Emerging Nebraska Poets.* Maritza will serve as the Editor-in-Chief of UNO's literary publication, *13th Floor Magazine*, in the 2017-2018 school year. Estrada was born in Toppenish, Washington, and has been living in Omaha, Nebraska, since 1999.

Deirdre Evans

Deirdre Evans, transplanted from Indiana to Nebraska in 1978, sank her roots in Omaha. She discovered slam poetry and the poetry community thirteen years ago. Her poetry has appeared in numerous Nebraska publications including *The Empty Room, The Untidy Season, UNO's Celebrate, the LOVE Book,* and *Fine Lines.* She is a board member of the Backwaters Press and a yearly judge for Poetry Out Loud. Aging hippie and anti-pipeline activist, she firmly resists the running dogs of the revisionist regime.

Marilyn Loy Every

Marilyn Loy Every holds a DMin, with a focus on aging, and Certifications in Spiritual Direction and Sage-ing Leadership. She also holds an MA in Counseling Psychology and MS in Audiology; she achieved a BS at the University of Nebraska. Marilyn is founder of Sagessence, a company with a mission to promote affirmative transformation of personal and cultural views that honor aging. She has authored *Fire in the Well, Women and the Liberating Journey of Aging,* and *Tending the Fire.* Marilyn was born and raised in Nebraska. She now lives in the Pacific Northwest where her love of nature and her love of family are her inspirations.

Kira Fish

Kira Fish has spent most of her existence living in a series of small towns across the state, and recently graduated from a state college with a degree in communications. Though not a ghost, she has friends who claim to have seen a few. She currently resides in eastern Nebraska.

Rodger Gerberding

Rodger Gerberding is a multidisciplinary artist active in applied arts, book illustration, writing, acting, and other venues. His painting, drawing, collage, and other multimedia work is represented by the Noyes Gallery (Lincoln, NE) and Gallery 72 (Omaha, NE); it has been exhibited throughout the Midwest and the east coast in one-person/group shows and has garnered a variety of awards. He has illustrated eighty books and, as a writer, has published four books to date, including *Come Now*, from Backwaters Press, and was nominated for a Nebraska Book Award; his poetry is represented in Backwaters' 20th anniversary anthology, *Watching the Perseids*.

Johnnye Gerhardt

Johnnye wrote a commercial that appeared during the Super Bowl; won an Omaha Ad Club Award; and a Certificate-of-Excellence Award for a Creative Training video. She studied screenwriting under Michael Hague, Professor Voorhees of the UCLA School of Film; Bob Anderson of New York; and graduated from the Superior Screenwriting Colony. Johnnye has written over 50 short stories, three novels, and ten screenplays. She's been an acquisition-and-contract editor for a small press. Johnnye serves on the Nebraska Governor's Education-Outreach Speakers Bureau; the Nebraska Film Association Board of Directors as Secretary; and served on the Nebraska Writers Guild Board.

Ellie Godwin

Ellie Godwin is a bookworm, first and foremost. She is also a volunteer, a traveler, and a sporadic photographer (when she happens upon something stimulating). Her photography has also been published in the literary magazine, *Xanadu*. She has lived her entire life in Omaha, Nebraska, and is a graduate of the University of Nebraska—Omaha. She currently lives in a happy home with her husband, Jake, and their yorkie, Mickey.

Victoria Goessling

Victoria Goessling has lived in Omaha most of her life, worked for over thirty years as a registered nurse, and spent part of that time in home care in the forgotten and misunderstood northeast section of Omaha. She's been lucky enough to meet a variety of interesting people. She travels extensively but always return to Omaha because, after all, it is home.

Ally Halley

Ally Halley grew up in rural Kansas and lived in Alaska and Turkey before settling in Omaha where she has lived for nearly twenty years. She is a financial analyst, mom, wife, and zombie enthusiast. As a pathological planner, she aspires to spend more time *living* life than planning it. Now that her sons are grown, she has been flitting from one long-forgotten interest to the next. She recently learned how to sing her favorite Italian aria and frequently belts it out, all alone, in her car. Creative writing is her latest foray into unadulterated joy.

Sheila Hansen

Sheila Hansen was born and raised a Nebraskan; she spent a good chunk of her childhood running amok on her grandparents' cattle ranches before moving to North Platte. After attending Hastings College, she moved to Lincoln where she currently works as a chiropractic assistant. When she's not working or writing, Sheila enjoys volunteering at the Lofte Community Theatre and judging speech tournaments for the Hastings College team or for local high schools.

Kellie Hayden

Kellie Hayden was born and raised in Omaha, Nebraska. She participated in one semester of a senior thesis program in poetry at the University of Nebraska—Omaha's Writer's Workshop. Her thesis focused on inheritance, or what and how we inherit from our family, as well as from our social and physical environments. Recently she has been reading about intergenerational trauma, focusing specifically on the "small violences" women inflict upon younger generations of women. Hayden served as Editor in Chief of UNO's literary publication, *13th Floor Magazine*, from January 2016 to July 2017, and briefly interned for The Backwaters Press.

Pat Hazell

Pat Hazell is not a born-of-the-husk Nebraskan. He spent his formative years on a steady diet of Goodrich Malts and Runzas, plotting ways to sneak into the Golden Spike Drive-in. He survived summers at the Cryer Pool, dances at Peony Park's Royal Grove and attended UNO for 90 days same as cash. Then he moved west to write for NBC's *Seinfeld*. He made seven *Tonight Show* appearances including one with fellow Nebraskan Johnny Carson. Pat serves as a creative consultant for film, television and stage. He is currently working on an original musical called *Grounded For Life*.

Heidi Hermanson.

Heidi Hermanson is a first-generation Nebraskan (born in Lincoln) with a lifelong love affair with Nebraska. She has been published in *Midwest Quarterly* and *Hiram Poetry Review*, and more recently, in the *North Platte Bulletin* newspaper, where she covered the astounding 2016 win of the Ogallala, Nebraska, Louder than a Bomb (a teen slam poetry festival) team.

Greg Kosmicki

Greg Kosmicki is a poet and retired social worker. Greg founded The Backwaters Press in 1997. Awarded the Jane Geske Award from the Nebraska Library Commission in 2011, the press published a poetry anthology in 2007, *Nebraska Presence*, which was selected as the 2018 "One Book One Nebraska." Author of thirteen books and chapbooks of poems, Greg was awarded two artist's fellowships from the Nebraska Arts Council. *It's as Good Here as it Gets Anywhere* (Logan House Press) was a 2017 Finalist for the High Plains Book Award. He and his wife, Debbie, are parents of three children, grandparents of two.

Justin Kruse

Justin Kruse is a Nebraska native originally from O'Neill, now living in Lincoln. For him, writing was always an afterthought to simply telling or remembering a story, until college. While he was working on his associate's degree at SCC, he took several composition and creative writing courses with professors who encouraged him to delve deeper into his skill with the written word. As a result, Justin now has a degree in English Education from Wayne State and sees writing as a potential future career, or at least as a hobby that lets him freely create without an entry fee.

Richard Kujath

Richard Kujath was born and raised in Southeast Nebraska. He graduated from Tri County High School, headed west, and landed in Phoenix, Las Vegas, Tucson, and other warm places. Also an honors graduate of Glendale (AZ) Community College, and a University of Arizona in Tucson grad with a BA in Literature. Married for nearly 35 years to a former Las Vegan, Kathy (Klingbiel) Kujath, they have two sons, Ricky and Joe. Both children were born in Arizona and raised in Nebraska. Richard and Kathy now live in Omaha, near their first and (so far) only grandchild. His poem, *Still,* was written for Richard's niece after the sudden, accidental death of her husband, and for his own therapy while his brother and sister-in-law were dying of cancer.

Samuel Lee

Samuel Lee was born in Minnesota, but moved to Lincoln, Nebraska, a few days later (not his idea), where he has resided ever since. He competes in poetry slams in Lincoln and Omaha, and is a teaching artist with the Nebraska Writers Collective. His work has been published in UNL's Laurus magazine and on Guacamole Lit Mag online journal. He also cooks at Leadbelly and can often be found arguing with somebody online.

Curt Liesveld

The late Curt Liesveld loved photographing the natural Nebraska beauty that surrounded his home. He was known to put on his boots and coveralls and tromp through fresh snow in order to capture the best of winter. Many of his photographs are now featured in his wife, Rosanne's, recently published book, *The Collision of Grief and Gratitude: A Pursuit of Sacred Light*.

Judy Lorenzen

Judy Lorenzen was born in Lincoln, grew up in Malcolm and Grand Island, and resides in Central City, Nebraska. She holds a BA, English; an MSED, Community Counseling (LMHP); MA, Creative Writing, all from UNK; and a PhD in Composition and Rhetoric from UNL. She teaches English in Grand Island. Her work has appeared in *Plains Song Review, Relief Literary Journal, Plainsong, Celebrate: A Collection of Writings by and About Women* (Volume XVI), *Nebraska Life* magazine, *The Fence Post*, and *The Untidy Season: An Anthology of Nebraska Women Poets*. Nebraska's beautiful prairies and pastures stole into her heart in her youth.

Jeanne Batten Lynch

Jeanne Batten Lynch, born in 1938, grew up on a Valley, Nebraska, family farm. She was the oldest child of George and Mary Batten. She had two siblings, Tom and Blaine. After graduating from country school, she attended High School in Fremont. In 1959, she married Dr. John J. Lynch, a professor of philosophy at Creighton University in Omaha. Later he taught at The College of the Holy Cross in Worcester, MA. They had three children, John III, Jeannie and Gregory. Jeanne graduated from the University of Massachusetts, and became a registered hospice nurse. She lives in Worcester, Mass.

Clif Mason

Clif Mason's poems have appeared or are forthcoming in many magazines in America and England and in *From the Dead Before*, a Lone Willow Press chapbook. His work has been awarded prizes by the Joe Gouveia Outermost Poetry Contest, *Writers' Journal*, *SPSM&H*, *Plainsongs*, the Midwest Writers' Conference, and the Academy of American Poets. His work has also been nominated for a Pushcart Prize. He is the recipient of a Fulbright Scholar Award to Rwanda, Africa. He lives in Bellevue, Nebraska, with his wife, a visual artist.

Robert Mundy

Robert Mundy is an attorney, a financial services planner, and president of Legacy Preservation, a company that helps businesses and families capture their histories through private publishing. He began focusing his efforts on writing fiction after reviewing movies for Midwestern newspapers for thirteen years. His stories have appeared in print and online journals since 2012. His collection of short stories, *I Fell from Earth and Slipped through the Cracks,* was published in the spring of 2017. He lives in Omaha, Nebraska.

Charlene Neely

Charlene Neely's poetry has appeared in many journals and anthologies. Her book *The Lights of Lincoln*, poetry and photographs of the fifty-one light bulbs that were part of a community-wide art project in Lincoln, Nebraska, was published in 2016. She enjoys sharing her love of poetry and words with people from three to ninety-three, give or take a few years either way. Born and raised in Nebraska, she has spent most of her life in Lincoln with interludes in several smaller towns in Southeast and South-central Nebraska.

Kathleen O'Brien

Kathleen O'Brien was born and raised in Nebraska. She became a Sister of Mercy and has lived and taught in several western states but always seems to come back to Nebraska. She has had several poems published in magazines such as *Sisters Today, Living Mercy, Metropolitan*: *Omaha's News, Opinion & Entertainment Weekly,* and Knowles Mercy Spirituality Center's web site. Kathleen has published three books about the Sisters of Mercy in the western United States as well as several articles in *Viva! Mercy!* She currently lives in Omaha and writes for children.

Frank S. O'Neal

Frank S. O'Neal is a poet and publisher. He has published four books of his surrealist poetry, and has performed pieces from coast to coast at poetry slams and book events. Nikki Giovanni endorsed his work, saying, "What a wonderful, emotional way to view the world! Dedication, Commitment. Honor. Frank is a great new voice, and we all should heed it." In the winter of 2017, The Nebraska Arts Council exhibited a new class of poetry, "Surrealist Poetry Video." The award-winning video, "I Do Not Use the N Word" was a collaboration between Frank and Nebraska Filmmaker, Jason Fischer.

Joe Pankowski

Joe Pankowski is an artist who is interested in dreams, machines, and capturing his daydreams with his sketchbooks. These drawings have spilled over into his paintings, films, gadgets, and installations which have been exhibited locally and nationally. Joe has taught drawing, painting, sculpture, and new media art as an art instructor throughout the Omaha Metro. He received his BFA from the University of Nebraska—Omaha with an emphasis in Intermedia, and his MFA in New Media Art from the University of Illinois at Chicago.

Chuck Peek

Chuck Peek's *Breezes on Their Way to Being Winds* won the 2016 Nebraska Center for the Book prize for poetry; Wayne State College Press published his *Where We've Managed Somehow to Be.* He grew up, lived, learned, and taught most of his life in Nebraska, and currently lives in Kearney. Twice the featured poet at the Buffalo Commons Storytelling Festival, he was also the reader for the Heartland Emmy Award-winning *Prayers for the People: Carl Sandburg's Poetry and Songs.* Peek served as a Fulbright Senior Lecturer in China and now teaches for Lincoln's OLLI program and Kearney's Senior College.

Charlene Pierce

Charlene Pierce was born and raised in Kearney, Nebraska, then earned a BFA from the University of Nebraska—Omaha, where she still lives. She is a member of Nebraska Writer's Guild, Fine Lines Writing Group, Chuck Writing Group, neighborhood book club, and Ladies' Poker Nights. Charlene is always surprised by where the characters in her writing take her and hopes the reader enjoys the journey as much as she.

Amy Plettner

Amy Plettner's great-grandparents settled in Fillmore County near Exeter, Nebraska, where both her parents were also born and raised. She considers Nebraska her home and never tires of its rich diversity. Her first book of poetry, *Undoing Orion's Belt*, is the 7th of the Kloefkorn series by WSC Press. She holds an MFA from the University of Nebraska. Amy's poetry has been published in a variety of journals and anthologies, most recently, *Nebraska Poetry: A Sesquicentennial Anthology 1867-2017, Bared* a *Les Femmes Folles Book, burntdistrict, Rattle*, and *The Untidy Season: An Anthology of Nebraska Women Poets.*

Douglas Polk

Douglas Polk is a lifelong resident of Nebraska. He is a poet who has had over 900 poems published in hundreds of magazines and websites. Polk was nominated for Pushcart awards in 2012 and 2013.

Bridgit Kuenning-Pollpeter

Bridgit Kuenning-Pollpeter is a graduate of the Writer's Workshop at the University of Nebraska. She's currently pursuing her MFA in writing from UNO. She has had pieces published in *Breath and Shadow*, *13th Floor*, *Omaha World-Herald*, and *Magnets and Ladders*. She blogged for Live Well Nebraska. She has edited publications for the National Federation of the Blind. She resides in Omaha, Nebraska, with her husband and two sons.

Gaylene Quinn

Gaylene Quinn joined a writing group in January 2016. She works in media and wanted to start writing fiction rather than just ad copy. Gaylene studied Business and Computer Science at Missouri State University, formerly Southwest Missouri State University, in Springfield, Missouri. She grew up in Norfolk, Nebraska, whose claim to fame is the home of Johnny Carson and the Great American Comedy Festival. Gaylene lives in Bellevue, Nebraska. Living on a golf course cinched a marriage proposal from her spouse, Ray. Gaylene enjoys gardening, reading, traveling and cooking, which happened recently once she discovered most people eat for enjoyment.

Chris Richter

Chris Richter was born and raised in Nebraska. She specializes in landscape photography, but is known to photograph anything that catches her eye.

Rhonda Rieck-Rush

Rhonda Rieck-Rush was born and raised in Nebraska, spending her younger years in tiny farm towns before moving to Lincoln as a teen in 1984 and graduating from Lincoln High in 1988. Rhonda writes poetry, prose, essay, and memoir, and is currently working on projects for future publication. Besides her passion for reading and writing, she is a nurse aid and self-employed caregiver. She'd relish the chance to take part in a writer's retreat or return to school for creative writing one day. Rhonda is a member of the Nebraska Writer's Guild.

Linda Robinson

Linda Robinson, 57, lives in Garrison, Nebraska, where she's lived all her life, except for a year when she worked out of town and a year spent in college in Omaha. She has four adult daughters and five grandchildren. She and her husband work for a small trucking company out of David City, Nebraska.

Todd Robinson

Todd Robinson has lived in Omaha his entire life, save for some childhood summers spent on a farm in Boyd county. He is a fifth-generation Nebraskan, and he has taught at three universities in our fair state. He is currently an Instructor in the Writer's Workshop at UNO, where you can visit his charming office (Weber 309) any time you wish. His poems have appeared in such venues as *Sugar House Review*, *UNO Magazine*, *Midwest Review*, and many other locales. Last year he completed a residency at the Kimmel Harding Nelson Center for the Arts in—where else—Nebraska City.

Lila Rose

Lila Rose moved to Lincoln, Nebraska, at the age of six. Storytelling interested her at a young age, creating picture books before learning to read. After her talent was noticed at eight, she took a few drawing classes and learned the basics of sketching. After college, she moved to Omaha where she still lives today. Later in life, Lila decided to teach herself to paint when planning her husband's wedding gift. She has been painting ever since. Lila is currently illustrating a few chapters of a novel she is writing, which she hopes to publish soon.

Marjorie Saiser

Marjorie Saiser, who grew up in north central Nebraska and lives in Lincoln, has received four Nebraska Book Awards. Saiser earned a Master's Degree in Creative Writing from the University of Nebraska—Lincoln. Her poems often deal with grassland, rivers, birds, and family, and a set of such poems have won the 2017 Fourth River Folio Contest. Saiser's poems have been published in *Prairie Schooner*, *Poetry East*, *Poet Lore*, *Nimrod*, *Rattle*, *Rhino*, and *Chattahoochee Review*. Poems of hers have been featured on the Writer's Almanac and in Ted Kooser's *American Life in Poetry*.

Barbara Salvatore

Barbara earned her BFA at the School of Visual Arts, New York City. Her art has been exhibited in New York and Nebraska and, along with her writing, been published in numerous literary journals and anthologies. Barbara is a student and teacher of the Ponca language, Plant Medicine and Horse Care.

Terry Lee Schifferns

Terry Lee Schifferns has been teaching writing and literature for twenty some years at a community college in central Nebraska. She has published in numerous literary journals. Her poetry is included in *Bison Poems*, *Jane's Stories*, *Times of Sorrow, Times of Grace*; and *Slamma Lamma Ding Dong*. She was awarded the Distinguished Artist of the Year in Literature by the Nebraska Arts Council in 2016. And she is still writing.

Donna Schluckebier

Donna Schluckebier teaches 2nd grade in western Nebraska where she lives with her boyfriend, three dogs, and three cats. Donna is not fond of cats, but is able to tolerate Ally, Meatloaf, and Karen just fine. Bo, Duke, and Riley ensure Donna gets plenty of exercise every day, and also hog most of her king-size bed each night. Her boyfriend, Chad, will propose sometime this century, after which Donna will finally acquire a shorter last name. Donna credits a killer sense of humor to the fact she has lived so long, as 1992 was quite a while ago.

Michael Skau

Michael Skau is an emeritus professor of English at the University of Nebraska—Omaha, where he taught from 1973 until retiring in August 2011. Skau has published poems in *Carolina Quarterly*, *Plainsongs*, *Midwest Quarterly*, and *Laurel Review*, among many other periodicals. He was named Winner of the 2013 William Kloefkorn Award for Excellence in Poetry, and his collection of poems, *Me & God*, was published by Wayne State College Press in 2014. His chapbook *After the Bomb* was published by WordTech Editions in July 2017.

Kim McNealy Sosin

Kim McNealy Sosin is a life-long Nebraskan. She grew up and graduated from High School in Humboldt, Nebraska, studied at the University of Nebraska—Lincoln, and was professor and department chair of economics at the University of Nebraska—Omaha until her retirement. Kim now enjoys travel, photography, and writing poetry. Her economics research was widely published, and more recently, her poetry and photographs have been published in several journals.

Bob Spittler

Bob Spittler, prize-winning longtime filmmaker and videographer at the Spittler Production Company, returned to still photography when he retired from advertising and commercial projects. While living in Tucson, his giclée photographic works were featured in several Arizona art galleries. His five panel giclée of Southwestern birds was selected for the Tucson Museum of Art 2008 Bicentennial show. Now back in Omaha, his nature photography is prominent in the coffee table books *Cowboys & Wild, Wild Things*; *The Desert Eternal*, and *The Legend of Brook Hollow*, and as illustrations for the essays and poetry of his wife, Connie.

Connie Spittler

Connie Spittler graduated from Creighton University. Her literary mystery *The Erotica Book Club for Nice Ladies* won a Eudora Welty Fiction Award from Washington, D.C., with international recognition from the Chanticleer Mystery & Mayhem competition and Wishing Shelf book clubs in Great Britain and Sweden, also published in the Czech Republic. Her essays appear in over 20 anthologies alongside notables like The Dalai Lama, Deepak Chopra, Barbara Kingsolver, Desmond Tutu, and Mikhail Gorbachev. Her illustrated nature essay book was a Southwest Book of the Year, and another essay book won Best Nature Book in NLAPW's bicentennial contest.

F. Patrick Stehno

Born and raised in Nebraska, F. Patrick Stehno jumped the Rockies into the Intermountain West at age 29, pursuing a career in geology. Educated in Omaha, he attended the University of Nebraska—Omaha, including the Community Writers Workshop. He was the Director of the Nebraska Poets Association, organized many public poetry readings for the local writing community, was the Coordinator of Programs and Service and later the Acting Director of the Metropolitan Arts Council, and conducted poetry residencies in several rural Nebraska high schools. Over the years he has had many poems published in literary journals, reviews, and anthologies.

Karen Heckman Stork

Karen Heckman Stork is the author of *Screw the Eggshells: Finding My* Self *After Verbal and Emotional Abuse* and producer and co-writer of *Between the Generations: Poems by a Nana and her Grandson*. She is currently a columnist for the *Lincoln 55Plus* senior quarterly newsletter with a column entitled "A Lincoln Life," and a blogger. Karen is a member of the Nebraska Writers Guild. She shares her story and speaks to groups on subjects including the harmful effects of verbal abuse, aging without growing old, life lessons learned, and poetry.

Max R.A. Thomas

Max R.A. Thomas is a 17-year-old first-time author on the autism spectrum. Her short stories, poetry, and prose are modeled after and influenced by Margaret Atwood, J.D. Salinger, Friedrich Nietzsche, and Sylvia Plath. She is a fierce advocate for the mentally ill, and enjoys research on theoretical particle physics, philosophy, and epidemiology. She loves to read literature from the Italian Renaissance and aspires to be a freelance writer whilst working at becoming a Nobel laureate in medicine for finding the cure for bipolar disorder. She lives in Bellevue, Nebraska, with her mother, father, sister, and two dogs.

LaVetta Vamosi

LaVetta Vamosi was born and raised in Omaha, Nebraska, where she continued to live for eighty blissful years, marrying the man of her dreams and raising three beautiful children and later being grandmother to seven amazing grandchildren. LaVetta had always been drawn to the arts, and in every form imaginable: painting, woodwork, stitching, stained glass—you name it, she dabbled in it. This very talented and beautiful soul left us this past February 4th, 2017. She is greatly missed, but her soul will live on in her many magnificent works.

Paula Wallace

Paula Wallace is a true farmer's daughter and has been making art since her days of Crayolas, Play-Doh and Etch-a-Sketch. Wallace graduated from the University of Iowa, with further training in Ireland and Chicago. In addition to fine art, Paula has worked as an illustrator and muralist, curator and arts facilitator, babysitter, waitress, summer parks and recreation staff, field worker, house painter, caterer and assistant to the executive chef, administrative assistant, library assistant, customer service representative, art instructor, floral designer, consultant, bookseller, customer order manager, set painter, and bartender. Her prior experience has qualified her for a position as an artist.

JOIN THE RANKS OF OUR AWARD-WINNING CLIENTS

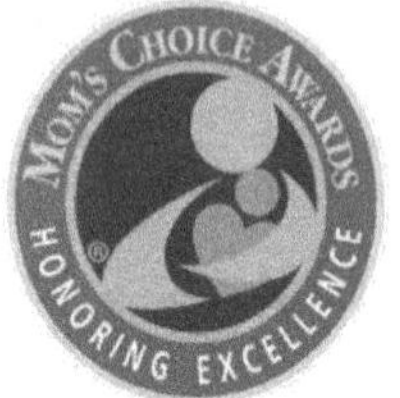

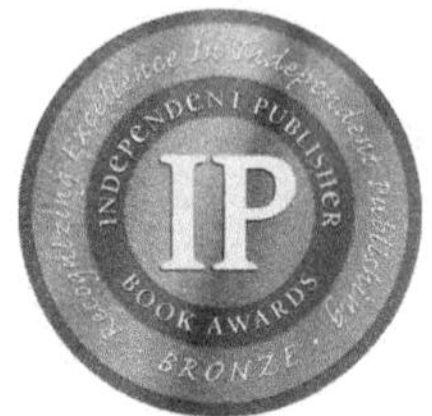

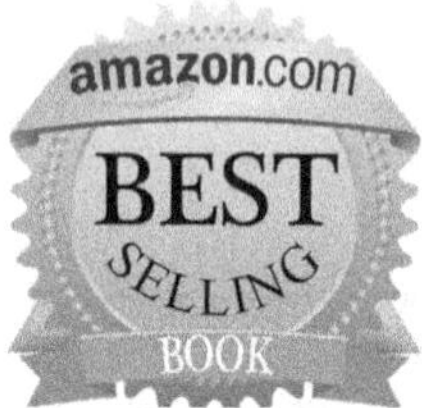

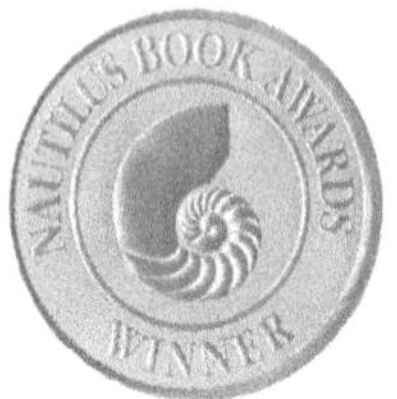

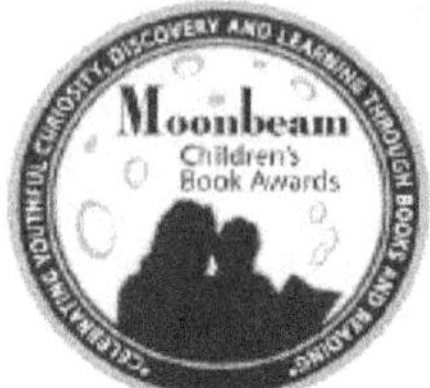

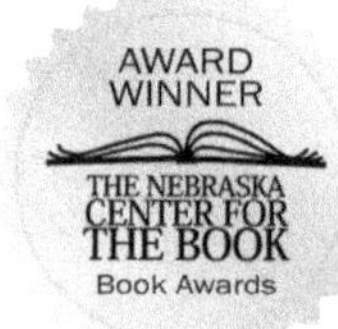

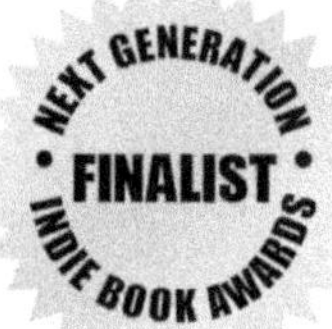

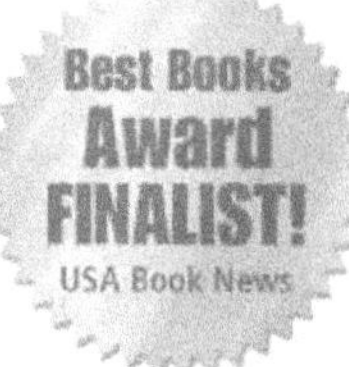

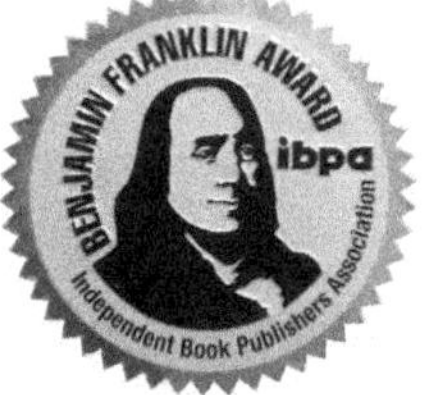

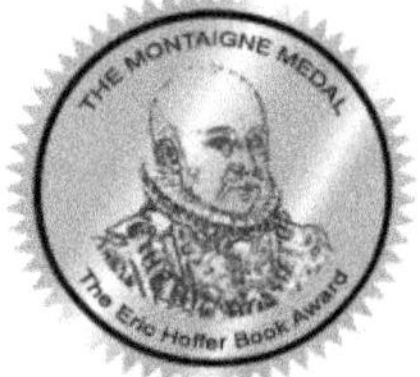

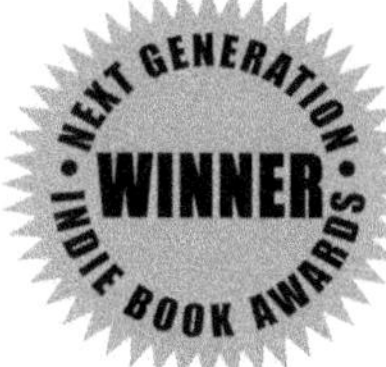

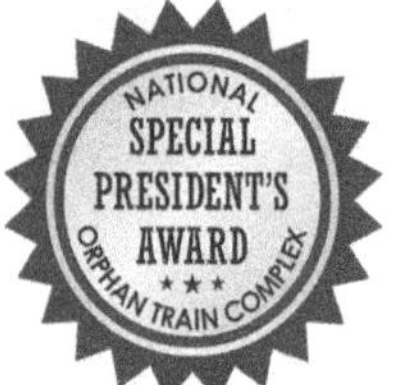

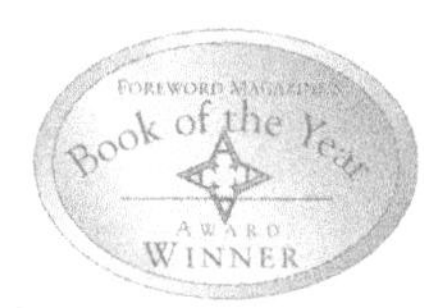

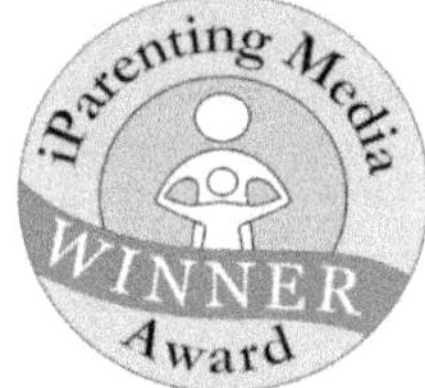

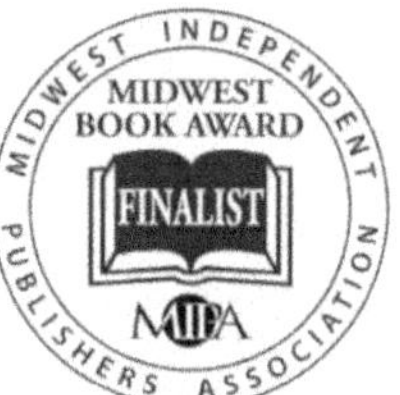

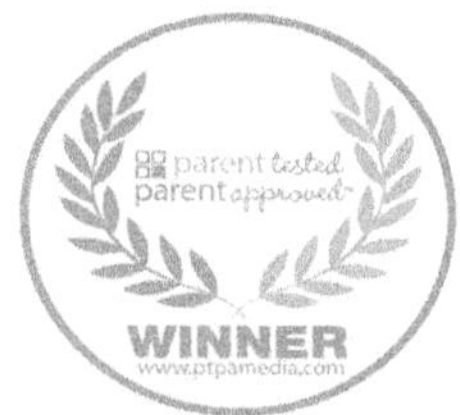

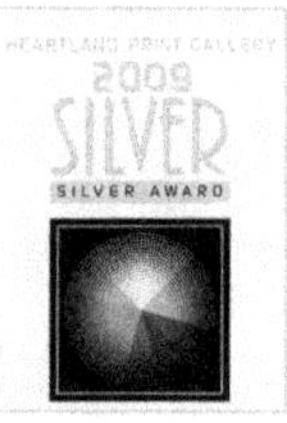

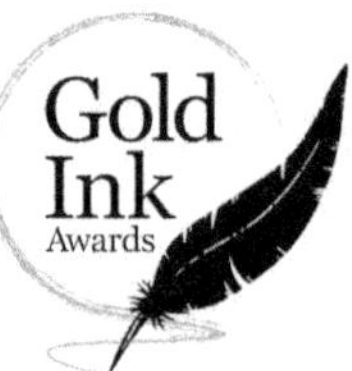

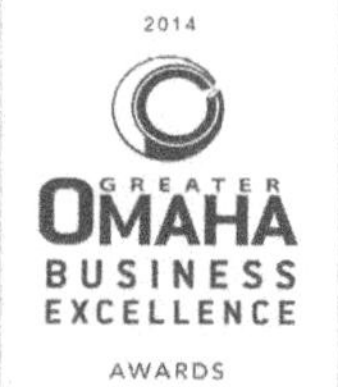

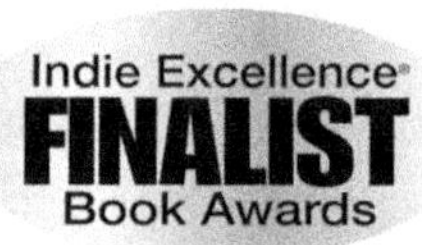

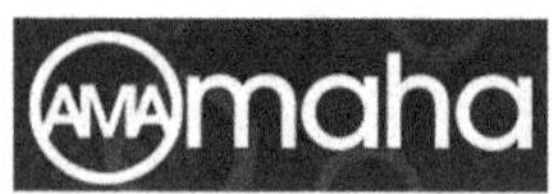

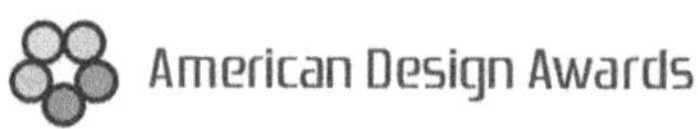

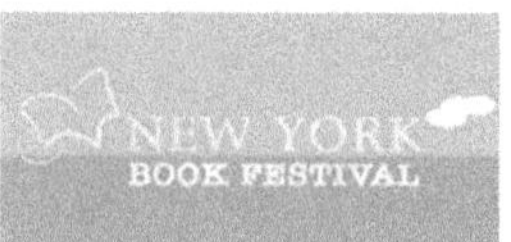

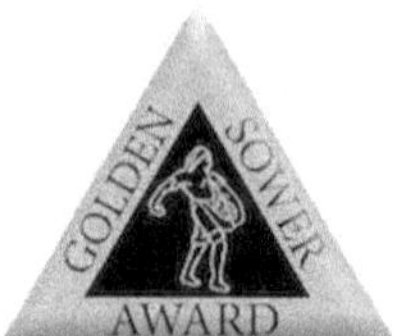

www.ingramcontent.com/pod-product-compliance
Lightning Source LLC
LaVergne TN
LVHW080330110826
845155LV00024B/143

* 9 7 8 1 9 4 5 5 0 5 5 8 4 *